Step-by-Step
PONDS, POOLS AND ROCKERIES

Step-by-Step

PONDS, POOLS AND ROCKERIES

PENNY SWIFT AND JANEK SZYMANOWSKI

First published in the UK in 1995
by New Holland (Publishers) Ltd
24 Nutford Place
London W1H 6DQ

Project coordinator Cherie Hawes
Editors Cherie Hawes and Richard Pooler
Designer Peter Bosman
Cover design Jenny Frost and Peter Bosman
Typesetting Deirdré Geldenhuys
Illustrator Clarence Clarke
Indexer and proofreader Hilda Hermann

Reproduction by Hirt & Carter
Printed and bound by Tien Wah Press (Pte) Ltd

ISBN 1 85368 538 0 (hbk)
ISBN 1 85368 539 9 (pbk)

The information in this book is true and complete to the
best of our knowledge. All recommendations are made without guarantee on
the part of the author and the publishers. The author and publishers disclaim any liability
for damages resulting from the use of this information.

CONTENTS

INTRODUCTION

For centuries, water has been a source of fascination and inspiration to people of all cultures, making it a common feature of garden design world-wide. This is not surprising since it introduces a magical, sometimes mystical element that is cleansing, cooling and restful. It can also captivate the senses, creating an air of excitement and adding a soothing or splashing sound. Whether your garden is large or small, new or well-established, water can add a pleasing and different dimension.

Ponds, pools and the myriad water features which go with them, are guaranteed to transform the most ordinary gardens and patios, giving them wonderfully magical and restful qualities. It does not matter what style, if any, you decide to follow or what impression you aim to achieve; when you decide to introduce a water feature into your garden, the possibilities are endless. And whether it is created in a formal, natural or a purely whimsical way, a well-planned water garden will give any outdoor area an aesthetic element which will be appreciated by all.

*The water lily (*Nymphaea spp.*) is the queen of aquatic plants.*

Generally, water has a tranquil and calming effect, but it will also bring both light and movement into a garden area. A reflective pond will quietly mirror images of plants, buildings and other features, highlighting colours and encouraging contemplation and a mood of calm, while a water course will tend to shine like a ribbon in the light of the sun or moon. Moving water, on the other hand, will splash and sparkle, producing varying degrees of sound and, often, an exhilarating air of excitement and anticipation.

In this book we illustrate a wealth of contemporary ideas for inspiration. While some projects are influenced by historical approaches, we have tried to present the widest range of possibilities imaginable. Building methods are discussed, and all the necessary equipment explained. There is also a section on fish and some valuable information about aquatics, oxygenators and other suitable pond plants.

In addition to the tried and tested techniques and methods used internationally to build ponds and other water features, we have included some innovative and unusual approaches.

Projects range from the simplest water feature, constructed using pre-cast materials, to formal ponds which require more demanding bricklaying skills. Whether you want to build an elaborate fountain or a simple duck pond, the instructions which follow will show you how. Where materials may be difficult to source, suitable alternatives are suggested.

A formal, circular fountain designed as a focal point in a parterre garden and originally laid out in the early 18th Century.

HISTORIC WATER GARDENS

Water gardens and features have been an important element of garden design since ancient times, frequently symbolising mystical and religious beliefs.

In Egypt, for instance, water was appreciated as the source of life for civilization, and irrigation systems were established for survival. Perhaps inevitably, water soon became a prominent component of the renowned pleasure gardens along the River Nile. Likewise, in Ancient Mesopotamia, ponds and running water were a feature of the historic gardens which were irrigated by the Euphrates River. In Persia (modern-day Iran), where gardens were traditionally identified with paradise, water was frequently the focus of attention. Here, tiled water channels were symmetrical and balanced, and believed to represent the unity of the universe.

Further east, in China, water and rocks represented the Oriental concepts of masculine and feminine, yielding yin and extremely powerful yang. They were the important elements of Chinese landscape architecture and expansive bodies of water were often created.

In Japan, where water is still valued for its tranquillity, ponds have always been quite commonplace. Even where there was no water, round stones were used to create imaginary rivers of life. Furthermore, modern Japanese gardeners and landscape architects are renowned for their ability to use even the smallest quantities of water to create beautifully delicate and inspired features.

In Byzantine times, the Romans were acclaimed for their canals and sophisticated water systems, and established magnificent water gardens, which were sometimes copies of the Egyptian designs.

Some of the world's most spectacular water features were devised in 16th and 17th Century Europe. Many of these may be still be viewed in well-maintained Renaissance gardens — at Villa d'Este in Tivoli, Italy, the spectacular Fountain of Neptune and impressive Pathway of the One Hundred Fountains are both celebrated landmarks. In the Austrian Alps at Schloss Hellbrunn near Salzburg, tourists are regularly entertained by the ingenious fountains and 'water games' installed by a prankish archbishop in the 17th Century. And in France, the hydraulics at the Palace of Versailles are marvels, where 1 400 fountains are operated by huge mills and pumps fed by the River Seine.

Then there are vast man-made lakes, some in the ancient Orient as well as those favoured by English landscape gardeners during the 18th Century. Of course, many of these features were simply dammed rivers and streams manipulated by grand gardeners like Capability Brown, to reorganize the landscape and reflect its beauty.

IDEAS AND INSPIRATION

While it is true that few can afford to accommodate the types of ponds, fountains and spectacular features found in the grounds of public buildings and large residences, many of these can serve as inspiration. Photographs in magazines and books are another good source, as are established gardens both public and private.

Books tracing the history of garden design and tradition are brimful with further examples, since there are a multitude of large formal pools and monumental fountains all over the world, especially in the grounds of public buildings or gardens of the wealthy. These books can be a valuable point of reference as well as a rich source of inspiration when planning your own water garden.

Some parks and civic amenities incorporate water gardens, fountains and features in their general plan. Alternatively, garden clubs and associations frequently organize

Water trickles over rocks into an attractive, natural-looking pond.

Lush planting softens the edges of a concrete water feature.

visits to places which you might not otherwise have the opportunity of seeing. These are usually advertised in local newspapers or magazines.

Some nurseries and garden centres arrange regular outings and hold seminars and workshops where amateurs can learn the basics of gardening in general, and often the specifics of water gardening.

But this is not always enough; you may find the greatest inspiration of all in Mother Nature herself. Even the most formal architecturally-planned pools should complement their surrounding features.

Informal ponds, in particular, will reflect nature, and this is where you are assured of getting some of the very best ideas. Look carefully at natural water courses and watch how streams cascade over rocks and boulders or trickle down adjacent surfaces. Observe the natural plant growth in and around pools and look carefully at how rockeries are formed without the help of human hands. Above all, examine where natural ponds and pools are found. By observing natural water courses, and implementing these features in your garden, you will soon be able to mirror the beauty of the environment in your own surroundings.

A rustic bridge crosses a man-made waterway lined with river stones.

An attractive concrete-lined duck pond incorporates an island and quaint wooden bridge.

PLANNING
Location

Careful thought and logical planning are the key to incorporating a water feature into any garden or patio. The amount of space you have available, gradient, the existence of rocks and established plants will all have a direct bearing on the layout of your scheme. Local conditions will also influence your design, and soil type may determine the method of construction chosen (*see* pages 20-28).

You will have to decide what size your water garden will be and whether you want a formal feature or something which will blend with the surroundings. Are you planning to keep fish? Do you want to attract other wildlife, like frogs and birds, to the pond? You may simply be seeking the opportunity to plant aquatics, bog plants, water lilies and so on, or to create a pretty cascade with water flowing between different levels.

Having decided what you want, you will soon realize that a vital factor of any water feature is its location. If a corner looks as if it *is* a pond, that is an obvious spot for a natural arrangement. You will find that areas with natural rocks and boulders are often perfect sites, as are slopes where plants will not grow. Unexciting, shady corners may also benefit from water features although trees can cause problems when they lose their leaves.

It is best to begin by drawing a scale plan of the garden or area where you plan to construct the water garden or feature. Sketch in everything from buildings, paved paths or patios and rocks, to mounds, hollows, trees and established shrubs. Even if you decide to transplant or remove some plants, a plan is a good starting point. Indicate the direction of prevailing winds and note areas which are particularly shady or sunny.

It may be helpful to sit in the garden or on a patio near to the site you think will be most appropriate. Try to visualise the finished feature before you start digging holes or building permanent structures.

Then consider the plan in more detail. Do you need to incorporate paving around the pond or perhaps a rockery to help soften hard edges? Will you need to terrace a slope or build steps to reach the feature? If you are likely to create a muddy trail when walking to and from the pool, you may have to consider pathways.

The choice of materials will depend on several factors ranging from basic design to budget. However, it is essential to maintain a visual link with the rest of the outdoor area and any existing theme in the garden as a whole.

SAFETY

Wherever there is water in the garden, safety factors should be considered. Toddlers and animals can drown in even the shallowest pool and if a dog cannot get out of the water, it may come to grief.

If you have children and small animals at risk, the simplest solution is to fence the pond. Unfortunately, this generally spoils the aesthetics of any pool or water garden. Alternatively, site it where access is limited; perhaps on a patio approached through doors which can be locked when adults are not present.

The only other solution would be to re-examine your exact needs and choose a feature with a concealed water source (*see* pages 76-79) or perhaps a very small, shallow pond which can be covered or drained whenever necessary.

The simplest water feature you can choose is a pre-cast bird bath.

An attractive well-planted koi pond established alongside a paved patio.

An unusual three-tiered fountain pours into an informal pond.

BUILDING BASICS

Essential tools for bricklaying include a spirit level and corner blocks.

You do not have to be an experienced builder to construct or install a water feature. There are various types of ponds which you can easily build yourself, as well as fountains and smaller features that take the minimum of time and effort, and very few skills. There are, however, certain basic building principles which should be completely understood, and several tried and tested methods of construction and installation which will simplify and expedite the projects you intend to tackle. It is also invaluable to have a thorough knowledge of the tools and materials available, as well as the ability to accurately quantify and cost what is needed.

TOOLS

While the tools required for any project will depend on the methods and materials used, there is some basic equipment which all do-it-yourselfers should have at hand. By using the correct tool for the job, you will not only simplify the project, but ensure that all structures are properly built. Before you start work, ensure you have an adequate tool kit.

Retractable tape measures are the handyman's best friend. A good quality steel tape with a locking mechanism will enable you to set out projects accurately and without assistance. It will be an invaluable aid when checking the depth of an excavated site and when working with wood.

Picks, spades and shovels are essential for excavating in-ground ponds and pools. A pick is indispensable if you are digging hard or heavy clay soil, while a shovel,

A spade is used for mixing concrete in a sturdy builder's wheelbarrow.

with its scoop-shaped metal blade, is useful for shifting sand and other building materials. A spade is the most common tool used for digging, as well as for mixing concrete, mortar and so on.

Wheelbarrows are an obvious aid when it comes to shifting excavated soil and transporting bricks and other materials. For minor projects and smaller pools, you can use a shallow gardener's wheelbarrow; a builder's wheelbarrow is more practical if you plan to use it for mixing mortar and small quantities of concrete. In any case, it makes sense to buy a good quality barrow with a pneumatic tyre.

Pegs are a practical aid for laying out ponds and artificial watercourses, and for establishing the upper levels around both formal and informal pools. You can buy metal pegs or make inexpensive wooden ones from a stout stick or post.

Compactors are worthwhile items when paving around a pond or pool, or when flattening the interior floor of a sizable water feature. While it is sensible to hire a mechanical compactor for a large project, especially if you are clay puddling (*see* pages 52-53) to seal it, or if you have to compact hardcore to form a firm sub-base for paving, a homemade punner or ramming tool will be adequate most of the time. To make one, either fill a five-litre (one gallon) tin with concrete and set a pole in the centre, or nail a solid block of wood to the end of a post and use this to flatten and compact the soil.

Levels of various kinds are used for just about every building project imaginable – even the simplest. First on the list of requirements is a spirit level which will help you ensure that everything, from brickwork and paving to bridges and even precast fountain features are flat, level and vertical. These fundamental instruments usually have two vials for both horizontal and vertical use. There are various sizes available, but 1.2 m (4 ft) is a handy length for most projects. If you find the spirit level is not long enough, you can always place it on top of a straightedge (*see* page 12), so that it can reach right across the pond or pool. Compact carpenter's squares (*see* page 11) also incorporate spirit level vials.

A *dumpy level* is a useful aid when level-ling the ground around the perimeter of a large water feature from a given datum point (the known level), or for determining drainage levels. The equipment is set up on a tripod a short distance from the pool, and a staff or pole, which has been insert-ed in the ground at the edge of the exca-vation, marked to indicate the level required. One person looks through the lens, which incorporates a spirit level vial, and visually lines up the datum point on a series of pegs inserted around the perime-ter. A second person marks off the pegs to show where the surrounding surface should be. Since these professional tools are expensive, it makes sense to hire rather than buy one.

Although relatively expensive, a dumpy level is a very useful tool.

A water level can be made fairly easily with inexpensive transparent tubing. To work efficiently, it is vital to ensure there are no air bubbles in the water.

A *water level*, which is among the least expensive tools of any builder's trade, is invaluable. Working on the principle that water finds its own level, it has a multi-tude of uses. When building a pond or pool, a level of this kind will enable you to accurately mark the surface area around the water, from a known datum point. Rather than using expensive professional equipment, all you need is a length of flexible transparent tubing and some water. When working alone, you can attach each end of the tube to a post and check the levels in this way; or ask a helper to hold one end in position and then move the other end of the tubing yourself, to establish the true horizontal level at other points around the pond.

Homemade corner blocks are ideal for keeping courses level when laying bricks. These are made by sawing a groove in L-shaped pieces of wood. Builder's line or string is then wound around two blocks (*see* illustration) which are then slotted onto each end of the brickwork.

Squares, made to form an exact 90° angle, are essential for checking corners, not only of formal pools, but also of regular step-ping stones and any other structures you may wish to include in the water feature. A *builder's square*, usually made of steel and considerably larger than a normal mathematical set square, is the most com-mon tool used for any building project. When laying out rectangular and square ponds a homemade square is useful. This

The simple water level is invaluable.

tool can be nailed together using three lengths of wood to form a right-angled tri-angle in the ratio 3:4:5. It may be as big or small as you wish, but the timber should not be warped, and you must be able to transport and handle it with ease. Three lengths measuring 900 mm, 1.2 m and 1.5 m (3 ft, 4 ft and 5 ft) work quite well.

A corner block and line in position.

You can level a circular pool by placing a spirit level on a straight piece of wood. Make sure all the outer pegs are level first.

A trowel is essential for bricklaying.

Carpenter's squares (or try-squares) usually made with one wooden and one metal side, sometimes have a spirit level vial for accuracy. Although these are too small for construction work, they may be used for smaller projects, as well as those which involve woodwork.

Straightedges are, quite simply, straight, even lengths of wood or light metal (aluminium for instance). It is easy to make your own – a spirit level, for example, may be used as a straightedge – or you can buy one. A straightedge has become one of the most important items in both a DIY and a professional tool kit and it is used for all kinds of building projects – in conjunction with a spirit level over an excavated hole or across a large area; to flatten building sand beneath paving; or it may even be used to level off a concrete slab. Marked off to indicate even brick courses plus a mortar joint, this tool may be used as a gauge rod during bricklaying.

Trowels are essential items in the tool kit of anyone building a brick or concrete shell. *A bricklayer's trowel* is used for spreading mortar, jointing paving slabs, and even for levelling small areas of concrete. A smaller trowel may be used to neaten the joints in the facebrick walls of a formal pool, although special pointing trowels are available; or you can use a piece of metal. *Rounded trowels*, which are used by contractors building hand-packed concrete and plastered swimming pools, are useful for smoothing the inside shell of rendered ponds (*see page 44*).

A *rectangular-shaped plasterer's trowel* is used to apply render or plaster to walls, and to float the surface of a plastered wall or floor screed when a very smooth finish is required. *Angle trowels* are invaluable for neatening both inside and outside corners of formal plastered ponds, and the supporting piers for stepping stones. *Notched trowels* are utilised for tiling.

A *wooden float*, which has a similar shape to a plasterer's trowel, is usually used to smooth the wet render after it has been laid on.

Hawks, which are used by most artisans, are useful for holding render and mortar when rendering or bricklaying. These tools, also known as mortar-boards, have a handle which is more convenient than the piece of flat metal or board usually chosen by most handymen.

Cutting tools of various types are required for many of the projects. You will need a pair of sharp, general-purpose *scissors* to trim plastic liners, an *angle grinder* or tile-cutting machine if you are finishing an edging or stepping stones with tiles, and a *saw* to cut wood. A *bowsaw* is useful for sawing logs and wooden poles, and a *tenon (or back) saw*, for most other small jobs. A *hack-saw*, which may also be used for cutting metal, is favoured by many DIY enthusiasts. An *electric jigsaw*, which will cut both straight and curved edges, is indispensable for those tackling the wooden bridge project on page 84.

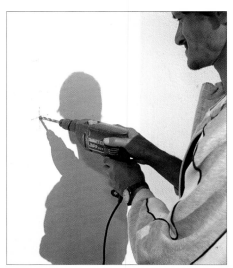

It is imperative to use the correct bit with your drill, depending on the material you are drilling.

The chisel end of a brick hammer or a brick bolster with its wide blade, will, as mentioned above, enable you to cut bricks to the required size or shape.

Hammers are tools which most people have, even if they are not DIY enthusiasts or particularly handy. The most useful is an ordinary *claw hammer*, designed for both

knocking in and extracting nails. A hefty *club hammer*, used in conjunction with a *wide-bladed cold chisel* (brick bolster), or the chisel end of a brick hammer, may be used to cut bricks. A *rubber mallet*, which looks rather like a hammer, has a heavy rubber head, and is useful for tapping paving bricks, blocks and pre-cast slabs firmly into position.

Screwdrivers and spanners are used for woodwork (building bridges, decking and so on) as well as for attaching some fountain fixtures and fittings to walls. Various *spanners*, including flat, socket and ring types, are required for tightening nuts and bolts, while screwdrivers are, of course, used for fastening screws. You can buy a set of screwdrivers, in different sizes, with both flat blades and cross-point drivers (for Phillips, Pozidriv and Supadriv screw heads). A *spiral ratchet screwdriver*, with interchangeable blades and drivers, is a good investment.

Wood screws and self-tapping screws which are described by number, are available in a wide range of lengths and diameters or gauges which are described by number. A number 6 screw, for instance, may be anything from 13 mm to 50 mm (½ in to 2 in) long, with a shank diameter of 3.5 mm (⅛ in). *Bolts* are described by their length and diameter.

Drills are not generally important for the construction of ponds and pools, although you will need one if you are incorporating wooden features or affixing a wall-mounted gargoyle on a fountain. Most DIYers will already have an electric drill which is more versatile than a hand drill (wheel brace), and you will be able to use it for a wide range of additional tasks. There is a large assortment from which to choose, but those with a variable speed are generally recommended. Models with a hammer action will enable you to drill into concrete, bricks and timber. Before you can use your drill, you will need a selection of masonry bits for drilling into brickwork and concrete, and a choice of wood bits for making holes in timber.

Sanders There is not much sanding to be done when building water features, and a sheet of a suitable grade sandpaper combined with a little physical effort, will usually suffice. However, both belt sanders, which will level slightly rough wood, and orbital sanders, for finishing, will prove invaluable if you are building wooden bridges or erecting decking. A carborundum stone is effective for smoothing the edges of cut tiles.

Polyethylene is an inexpensive material which can be used to line ponds.

MATERIALS

Bricks and mortar, rocks and concrete, clay or even a simple plastic liner can all be used to build a water feature. Various precast units may be used as fountains, and there are ready-made ponds available which can be sunk into the ground. Timber may be utilised for bridges, decking and jetties, and there is a wealth of other materials available to surface the surround of your pool. Various factors, including your building skills, budget, and the effect you want to achieve, will influence your choice.

Sodium clay

Clay puddling is one of the oldest methods of creating an impermeable lining for ponds. Since few sites have suitable clay-rich soil naturally present, it is usually necessary to bring this in. To ensure the pond will be watertight, an impervious clay must be used. Alternatively, a montmorillonite or sodium clay like bentonite can be used.

Found in isolated pockets all over the world, bentonite is used in industry worldwide, from heavy construction and the foundry industry to wine making, where it is used as a clarification agent. This natural clay is processed and packaged in powder (or sometimes granular) form, specifically for the sealing of reservoirs and dams. It is

not generally available from builders' merchants; you will need to locate a specialist supplier. Alternatively, you may be able to buy 'puddle clay' from clay suppliers.

If minor cracks occur, or if the shell is punctured, the clay will move into the hole and repair it with no effort on your part.

This makes bentonite suitable for sealing fish ponds of all sizes, big and small. Another advantage is that it may be used with all types of soil, although if you have clay on site, you will need less bentonite than if it is sandy.

Sealing a pond in this way is reasonably straightforward and requires no special skills, but it is essential to follow the correct procedure (see page 20). If you do not, the pond may leak which, in turn, could result in the exposed clay drying out and eventually cracking.

One golden rule that should never be broken is to avoid using bentonite in wet weather, or even if rain threatens. Once the soil and bentonite have been compacted, it takes a couple of days for the water hydration process to take place, and for the material to swell fully.

Bentonite matting is another product which can be used to seal ponds. It is, however, a more expensive and less usual method. This material is not widely available in the majority of countries.

Flexible liners

Various kinds of flexible liners are invaluable for the waterproofing of ponds and pools. Not only may they be used for just about any size or shape of pond, but also to establish a bog garden or even to line a cascade or waterfall.

Polyethylene is the most inexpensive type of flexible liner which, although widely available, is much maligned because it punctures relatively easily and deteriorates when exposed to the sun's ultra-violet (UV). Commonly used for damp-proofing various parts of buildings, it is manufactured in various colours and different gauges. Black sheeting contains carbon which inhibits the effect of UV light and increases its lifespan, making this colour the obvious choice for ponds. Fortunately, black pools also look more natural.

Since it is an accepted fact that exposed polyethylene will become brittle and eventually degrade, it is best to lay pavers around the perimeter of the pond so that they overlap the water slightly, providing some protection from the sun. Also keep the pond topped up so the liner is constantly under water.

While it is quite possible to line a pond with relatively thin, 250 micron polyethylene, there is no doubt that 500 micron will last longer; and some experts even advise using the thicker plastic as a double layer.

Recycled polyethylene should be rigorously avoided as it does not have the strength of virgin plastic.

A cross-laminated, high density polyethylene, may be used with rubberised asphalt, which acts as an adhesive, to join (or even patch) this type of plastic. It is manufactured in sheets for waterproofing various parts of a building.

PVC or vinyl sheeting, commonly used to line swimming pools, is the second option. Normally considered more UV stable than polyethylene, it is most commonly manufactured in blue or black.

As it can be heat welded in the factory, PVC is suitable for quite large pools, and is sometimes packaged in kit form.

Like polyethylene, PVC may be punctured by sharp objects, and it is also affected by the sun. Although PVC itself does not stretch, the addition of plasticisers during the manufacturing process makes some PVC liners relatively elastic. This makes it easier to gradually smooth out crinkles and wrinkles as you fill the PVC-lined shell with water.

Laminated PVC, which may be produced in tarpaulin grades, incorporates textile reinforcing which gives it strength.

Although it is commonly used as a pond liner in Britain, this application is not customary throughout the world.

Woven polypropylene, another type of plastic, is quite long-lasting and may be used to line ponds. More commonly used for erosion control, this matting material may be draped in the excavated hole and then coated with a rubberised bitumen sealer to make it completely waterproof. Unlike other liners, it cannot be used for ponds unless it is sealed.

For concrete, the cement and sand are combined first (top) and then they are mixed with water, before the aggregate is added.

Butyl rubber is undoubtedly the most expensive flexible liner, but one which the experts say is highly resistant to puncturing and degeneration as a result of UV rays. Normally black in colour, it is said to have a life expectancy of at least 50 years.

Although it has various applications, butyl rubber has been used for half a century to line canals and reservoirs in some countries. If it is used for a pond, it should be at least 0.75 mm (½ in) thick.

EPDM, an ethylene propylene polymer, has taken the place of butyl in some countries. A cheaper rubber, it is also UV-resistant and thought to be long-lasting.

Rigid liners

The range of pre-cast ponds and rigid liners varies in different areas. The most common materials used for construction are fibreglass, fibrecement and various thermoplastic materials. Glassfibre reinforced cement ponds are a relatively new invention and not available world-wide; small features are moulded into various shapes, while panels may be used together with a thermoplastic or butyl rubber liner.

Fibreglass (glassfibre reinforced polyester) may be moulded to any configuration and used to create both formal and informal ponds. Made by bonding several layers of glassfibre with polyester resin, these pools may be made in virtually any colour, although availability will depend entirely on the manufacturers in your area. They are invariably the most expensive option in this category of pond.

Fibrecement, like fibreglass, may be moulded to virtually any shape. Although there is a wide selection of plant containers, there are few configurations of pond available, and the material itself is not common in all countries.

Made of a mixture of organic fibres, cement, and sometimes a small percentage of asbestos, fibrecement is lighter than pre-cast concrete, but considerably heavier than fibreglass.

Thermoplastic shells are made from a variety of related materials including PVC and polypropylene. Demand probably regulates availability (they are common in Britain where numerous different designs are manufactured).

Glassfibre reinforced cement (GRC) is a relatively new product (see page 94). Instead of using a resin with glassfibre to make a fibreglass shell, or cement with natural fibres to form fibrecement, glassfibre is combined with cement to make it rigid. While it is only available from specialist outlets and actual methods of manufacture may vary, this is an effective material, not only for natural preformed ponds, but for very realistic fake rocks as well. Moulded to form panels, it can be used to support a vinyl-lining.

Concrete

This multi-purpose material has a multitude of applications. It is used for foundations, to build some pool shells, as well as arched bridges and the footings for wooden decking set in the water. It is also useful for supporting paving around the edge of some ponds (see page 26).

Concrete is made, quite simply, by mixing ordinary Portland cement, sand, and a coarse aggregate (crushed stone or coarse gravel) with water. Although it will be reasonably impermeable if a waterproofing compound is added to the mixture, concrete shells should also be rendered (see Bricks and Blocks, page 15) and coated with polyurethane or a bituminous waterproofing compound.

While cement is commonly sold in 50 kg bags or pockets, sand may be purchased in bulk or in 40 or 50 kg (88 or 110 lb) bags filled by builder's merchants. The best quality sands are evenly graded and contain particles of various sizes, and a reasonably coarse or 'sharp' type (up to 4.75 mm or ¼ in) should preferably be used for concreting. Although the actual source of the sand is not a reliable guide to its quality, in general you will find that most natural pit or river sands are suitable for concrete work. Specially manufactured crusher sand, which is washed and graded, may also be used.

Like sand, aggregate, which is generally graded to a 'single-size', is sold bagged or by volume. Although quantities in this book are given for 19 mm (¾ in) stone, you may find it easier to work with a smaller 13.5 mm (½ in) aggregate if mixing by hand. If natural pebbles are available in your area, these may also be used, provided they are of a suitable size.

Packs of dry-mixed concrete are available at most major hardware outlets. Although more costly than buying the necessary materials individually, these may be more convenient for people tackling minor projects which call for small quantities of cement, sand and stone.

While sand and stone are easily stored outside under plastic or a tarpaulin, cement should rather be stacked indoors, preferably on a platform to prevent it getting wet and hardening. Discard lumpy cement as this indicates it has been exposed to moisture. If you can break the lumps up easily, or sieve them out, you can use it for minor garden projects; do not be tempted to use inferior quality cement to build a water feature.

The water used to mix concrete should be clean and fresh. A rule of thumb is that if you can drink it, you can use it.

Various grades of concrete are used for different projects, depending on their type and magnitude. While medium- and low-strength concrete is suitable elsewhere in the garden, watertight walls and pond foundations should be built from a high-strength 1:2:2 mixture of cement, sand and stone. Adjust this ratio to 1:2:1.5 if you are using the smaller-sized aggregate.

Bricks and blocks

Made from burnt clay or pre-cast concrete, bricks and blocks may be used for the walls of formal pools and, if you wish, for the surrounding paving. Both types come in a range of colours from charcoal to terracotta, and the laying procedure is the same, regardless of size.

If you are building walls, your immediate decision will be whether to render the brickwork, to use low-maintenance face-bricks or reconstituted stone blocks and to leave the walls unrendered.

Whatever you decide, you will need mortar, made with cement and sand, for bricklaying and possibly for jointing paving bricks or slabs. If you decide to render (plaster) your brickwork, cement and sand will be required for the render mixture.

Some ordinary building sands are suitable for mortar, but not the coarse sand that is normally used for concrete. In general, sand used to make mortar for bricklaying and rendering should be softer and finer than either the bedding sand laid under brick paving, or that used to make concrete. Maximum particle size should be no more than 2 or 3 mm (just a fraction of an inch). All sand should be free of clay, salt and vegetable matter. A good mortar mix for water features consists of cement and sand combined in the ratio 1:3.

Note that while it is usually considered good building practice to add hydrated builder's lime to render to improve its plasticity and help prevent future cracking, this should be avoided when building ponds. Lime is toxic and can kill fish and other creatures. You can, if you wish, add a non-toxic plasticiser to the mixture to make it more cohesive. A waterproofing additive will make the render coat more impervious to water (see page 17).

Although swimming pool builders frequently use marble plaster mixed 1:3 with white cement to give the shell a nice, smooth waterproof finish, this is an expensive and therefore infrequent option for fish ponds. Marble plaster is usually available in 25 kg (50 lb) bags.

If you decide not to coat the rendered pond with bitumen, it is best to fill and empty the feature several times before introducing plants or fish, to get rid of any traces of toxic lime (from the cement). Neutralizing chemicals may also be used.

Pre-cast concrete materials

Various pre-cast materials may be used when constructing water features.

Pre-cast concrete products, which range from ordinary paving slabs to ornamental fountains, can be extremely useful when constructing water gardens and features.

A small but classical fountain is set in a shallow, circular pool.

When paving around the perimeter of a pond or pool you can choose from concrete bricks, plain slabs and even interlocking units. Particularly popular are pavers, flagstones and setts (sometimes called cobbles), as well as imitation sleepers and fake log slices, all of which are made from reconstituted stone. Compressed or vibrated in moulds, these simulated stone products have an attractive appearance and are especially well suited to the more natural type of water feature.

Pre-cast fountains may be as plain or ornate as you wish, although those incorporating statuary are frequently used as a focal point in formal pools. Simple bird bath designs, manufactured from fibrecement as well as pre-cast concrete, may also be used as fountains. The majority of concreteworks will incorporate pipework in the mould to adapt them if necessary, while fibrecement is generally easy to drill into (see page 68).

Fake fibreglass or GRC rocks are also useful when building a water feature. They are considerably lighter than the real thing, and may be used to camouflage the pond edge, to hide pumps, filters and so on, and even to construct rockeries for waterfalls (see page 54).

A charming little pond, brimful with water plants, on a tiled patio.

Stone

A suitable material for use both in and around water features, stone comes in various guises. While boulders are the ideal choice for rockeries, natural and even reconstituted (or simulated) stone slabs are a common paving material around ponds and pools. A raised pond or bridge may be constructed from cut stone, and stepping stones created with reasonably flat rocks.

Stones can make a very effective edging around an informal pond, especially if you have some which stick out of the water, perhaps linking the pond to a pebble beach or bog garden.

When it comes to paving, an advantage of using man-made products is that they are reasonably regular in shape and size and therefore easier to lay. However, natural stone will blend with the environment more easily. Flagstones are relatively expensive and often difficult to find, but irregular pieces of cut stone or slate may be laid as crazy paving around ponds.

Another alternative is to use cobbles or setts (where available). Traditional setts were made from granite, and you can now buy concrete 'cobbles', which are flatter and more regular than water-worn stones taken from river beds. Of course, river stones are visually effective around a pond, but are not practical if you intend to use the area for sitting, as they create an irregular surface ill-suited to moveable furniture.

For a Japanese-style feature, pebbles and crushed stone or gravel are the perfect complement for water. You may use these materials to create a beach alongside the pond, or even as a method of camouflaging the concrete or plastic liner in the water. Your local garden centre should stock bags of these materials, although stone and gravel may also be obtained from suppliers of aggregate intended for building work or paving.

If you do have access to local stone, either from your own property or from a nearby quarry, this is usually the best option for rockeries, as it will help to create a most authentic effect.

Tiles

Suitable for patio surfaces and formal pool surrounds, tiles may be used around the edge of a pond or on top of stepping stones (*see* page 86). Since glazed tiles become extremely slippery and therefore dangerous, use those that are intended for outdoors and make sure they have a matt finish. Terrazzo, terracotta and quarry tiles are all suitable. If yours is a formal pool and your budget allows, you could always consider punched (rather than polished) marble tiles which are non-slip.

Timber

Although not the most common material used to construct ponds and pools, timber should not be overlooked. Most hot tubs, which like spas are fitted with a filter, heater and jets, are constructed from timber (Californian redwood for instance), so there is no reason why this material should not be used for ponds.

Wooden wine barrels make attractive and watertight containers. Like hot tubs, they are made from timber which is resistant to rot and which swells when wet. Note that barrels which are not used for winemaking will usually have to be sealed to make them watertight.

Hardwearing railway sleepers may be used to line the sides of a pool, or to build the entire structure. However, these will not be waterproof unless the interior surface of the pond is sealed with bitumen or fibreglass, or the excavation is first covered with a flexible liner.

Of course, timber is also a useful material for those special features which add the finishing touches to any water garden: bridges, adjacent decks, gazebos and jetties are all easily constructed from either poles or planks. Even though wood tends to get slippery in wet weather, it may be used as a flooring material for adjacent patios and as an edging for your pond.

Timber decks are particularly well suited to water gardens as the material blends well with the environment. While decking may be used successfully on both flat and sloping ground, to create terraces or simply to extend over a pond, a charming ploy is to allow water to flow under a deck to create the impression of a much larger feature than really exists.

Where part of the supporting structure of decking (or a jetty) is in the water, additional steps must be taken to ensure it is safe. You will have to treat wood that will remain submerged and piling may be required to anchor it securely. If necessary, consult an engineer who will design the foundations of the structure.

Wood can be bought as poles and split poles, or as sawn timber which may be rough-cut or planed all round (PAR). In addition, laminated beams, manufactured by gluing strips of wood together under pressure are available. These are usually expensive, but very stable and come in fairly long lengths.

While knots are unavoidable in various types of wood, it is best to avoid planks and boards with large knots as these can affect the strength of any structure.

Whatever you are building, it makes sense to use a wood that will last, and it is vital that the timber used for bridges and decks will not warp and split when it comes in contact with water. Although your choice will be limited to what is available in your area, you will find that hardwoods (*see* following page) are generally more resistant than softwoods (*see* page 94). One exception is Californian redwood, a softwood which is valued for its resistance to decay and infestation.

Some of the most popular species of hardwood include oak, which is attractive, strong and versatile; Philippine mahogany, another particularly durable wood; and, in hotter climates, balau, a fine-textured timber noted for its strength and durability and karri, a tough eucalypt which originated in Australia.

Nowadays, most sawn timber is treated with either organic or water-based preservatives, and is impregnated under extreme pressure in the sawmill. The actual chemicals used vary and some may be toxic to fish. However, a thick coating of hot tar or bitumen will protect the wood and seal in the poisons.

Although hardwood poles (which may be machined to size) are often dipped in creosote which is an oil distilled from coal tar, softwood poles like pine are more commonly treated under pressure with a water-based preservative like chromated copper arsenate (CCA). This may give the wood a slightly green tinge. While it is essential to buy timber that has been treated against infestation and rot, do investigate the poisons involved. Creosote is highly toxic and should be avoided.

Whatever wood you decide to use, store it indoors if at all possible. If not, it is advisable to stack it level at least 300 mm (1 ft) above the ground and to protect it with plastic or a tarpaulin to prevent it getting wet and warping or rotting before construction begins.

Metal

Although metal is often used to build public bridges, it is not common for ordinary gardens. In some situations, it can be used if combined with wooden slats. Apart from nuts, bolts, screws and other connecting mechanisms made from metal, reinforcing will also be required for some ponds and supporting wall structures. Although ordinary chicken wire (with its characteristic hexagonal mesh configuration) may sometimes be used, a more sturdy weld mesh is more frequently recommended. Sold in a roll, it can be cut to reinforce irregular shapes.

Since water is a constant factor, it makes sense to use metal that will not rust. Stainless steel, aluminium and galvanized or anodised metals are all suitable.

Waterproofing materials

There are various ways to ensure water features will be impervious and it is advisable to familiarise yourself with the full range of waterproofing methods.

Both flexible and rigid liners are waterproof, while concrete and brickwork are porous. Rendering the internal surface will make it reasonably watertight, especially if a waterproofing additive is included in the mix. There are several types available and it is important to follow the manufacturer's instructions to obtain good results.

Although not a common choice for ponds, one of the finishes for modern-day swimming pools is marble plaster which gives the shell a smooth, waterproof skin. Made from white cement and granular marble dust (mixed with water in the ratio 1:3), marble plaster is more expensive than ordinary render and known to be adversely affected by certain environmental conditions. Like any plaster, it must be sealed or treated with a neutralising chemical if you wish to keep fish.

Another possibility is to build a concrete or brick shell and to then make it watertight with a flexible liner or more costly fibreglass which is coated onto the surface *in situ*. The latter option, which may also be used to seal timber, is recommended where boulders and rocks are to be incorporated in the pond design.

Bitumen is one of the most common and least expensive sealants used by pond builders. Since it is black, it gives the pond a natural appearance. Choose a rubberised product which is water-based and non-toxic. Even if the pool has been rendered, this multi-purpose waterproofing compound is worth using as it will also prevent toxic lime from seeping into the water.

Moisture-curing polyurethane, available in different colours, including blue and black, may also be used to waterproof ponds. Products developed for use in tanks and dams containing drinking water and fish are tough, chemical resistant and non-toxic. You may need a specific primer, and may have to leave the pond to cure for a few days before filling it with water.

Various paints suitable for swimming pools may also be used. These may be either rubber-based, epoxy-based, vinyl-based, or acrylic.

Where holes have been drilled in walls to accommodate electric cables, use a suitable silicone sealer to prevent leaks.

Silicone sealer is successfully used to seal around an electric cable.

An unusual pool under construction was built with hand-packed concrete which was marble plastered prior to lining it with loose-laid bricks.

QUANTIFYING AND COSTING

Before you begin building or installing your water feature, it is sensible to ascertain exactly how much it is going to cost. While many of the items required may simply be priced at the source of supply, some materials will have to be quantified for the specific project before you can calculate costs. Some useful guidelines are detailed in this section.

Remember that you will need to order slightly more of certain of the items to allow for waste and breakage. In the step-by-step projects, quantities have been rounded off where appropriate. An additional percentage has not been included.

Bentonite

Where available, it is usually sold in powder form in 40 kg (88 lb) bags. Bentonite is generally mixed with soil and spread dry over the sloping walls and floor of the pond. The ideal soil type is clay, in which case you will need approximately 5 kg (11 lb) for every square metre (10 sq ft) it must cover. Sandy soil should be mixed with as much as 8 kg (18 lb) to cover the same area.

Estimating the quantity of soil required can be problematic. It is reasonably safe to work on a soil weight of 1.75 kg for every litre (3 lb 11 oz per 2 pints) or 0.001 m³ (0.035 cu ft). This means that for every square metre to be sealed, you will need approximately 175 kg (386 lb) of soil to mix with the bentonite.

If a pure blanket of bentonite is spread over the pond basin, you will need considerably more of this material. In most instances, 10 kg (22 lb) will be sufficient to cover 1 m² (10 sq ft).

Flexible liners

Unless your pool is a reasonably regular shape, you will find it necessary to buy very much more liner than you actually need to form a blanket over the excavation. Unfortunately, there is very little you can do about this waste.

For minimum waste, it is essential to ascertain the dimensions of various liners during the planning stages. The maximum width of polyethylene varies, depending on the gauge; the thinner the sheeting, the wider it may be. While some types of sheeting can be joined, be cautious, it may not last. EPDM, for instance, is very difficult to bond. PVC can be heat welded in the factory, so although you cannot join it yourself, you may be able to order a custom-made pool liner to fit.

Another solution is to find out what is readily available in your area, and, if necessary, adapt the size of the pond to suit the liner you have chosen.

To ascertain how much material you need, draw the pond roughly to scale, and measure its length and breadth at the longest and widest points. Decide how deep it will be, and add twice the depth, plus a bit extra for around the outside edge, to both the length and the width. Rather buy too much material than find later that you do not have enough.

Concrete

To work out the quantities of cement, sand and stone required for your concrete mix, it is necessary to estimate the total volume of the foundations and/or the concrete shell, using the simple mathematical calculation: total area x thickness. Since most pool walls are fairly low, a 100 mm- (4 in-) deep foundation trench is usually quite adequate, while a concrete shell will be at least 80 mm (3 in) thick. Remember that the length and width of foundations are always slightly greater than the dimensions of the wall or structure it supports.

Presuming you are mixing cement, sand and crushed stone in the ratio 1:2:2, you will need approximately eight pockets (400 kg/880 lb) of cement and 810 kg, (0.6 m³/21 cu ft) each of sand and aggregate, as well as sufficient water to produce a workable mix, for every 1 m³ (35 cu ft) of concrete.

Bricks, blocks and tiles

Brick sizes do vary slightly, but most are about 222 mm (8¾ in) long, 106 mm (4 in) wide and from 50 mm (2 in) to 75 mm (3 in) thick; the thinner bricks being for ordinary domestic paving. Blocks used for building and slabs utilised for paving are less standard; these sizes depend on the individual manufacturer.

When calculating the number of ordinary bricks required for a wall, it is safe to assume you will need 55 for each square metre of half-brick walling (46 bricks per square yard), that is 106 mm (4 in) thick. For every square metre of brick paving, you can count on using as many as 45 pavers (38 per square yard).

Alternatively, simply estimate the surface area of each building unit and the approximate area of your proposed wall or paved surface; divide the first figure into the second and you will immediately know how many to buy.

The easiest way to quantify pre-cast blocks or slabs and tiles, is to calculate the area of a single unit and then divide this into the total area to be paved. If you are using flagstones or pavers of varying sizes, the simplest solution is to add together the areas of each kind and use equal numbers of every sort of paver.

Stone

Unlike man-made products which are of standard sizes and therefore reasonably easy to quantify, it is more difficult with rocks and stones, and you may have to enlist the help of professionals.

The availability of natural stone directly affects its price. If you are fortunate enough to have rocks and boulders on site, these will cost you nothing. If there is a quarry in your area, it is advisable to get rocks directly from there. Although transportation can be costly, it is likely to amount to less than if you were to buy from your local garden centre or through a professional landscaper.

In general, stone is classified according to its finished surface: it may be rockfaced, rough picked, axed, split or sawn.

Mortar

The quantity of mortar required for brick-laying depends on the cement:sand ratio, and the size of the brick or block you are using. Since a reasonably strong 1:3 mix is recommended for this type of work, you will need approximately one pocket of cement and 155 kg (340 lb) of sand for every 150 bricks laid in a half-brick wall.

The same mix may be used for render, and, provided it is spread evenly to approximately 10-15 mm (about ½ in) thick, the above quantity will enable you to render about 7 m² (75 sq ft) of wall.

Remember that the standard of your bricklaying and plastering skills will have a direct effect on the amount of waste of these materials. If you work neatly and cleanly, the estimates found in the following projects will be fairly accurate.

Timber

Standard sizes of timber are reasonably universal, although you will find some variation. In general, metric sizes are simply conversions from the imperial system which was established in Britain many years ago. In Europe these measurements have been rounded off, while in certain other countries, including South Africa, the exact conversions are still used.

When ordering timber, it is not essential to buy the dimensions identical to those specified for projects, provided they are similar. It is more sensible to get what is available at your local sawmill or timber merchant than to have the wood specially planed to size.

Similarly, the lengths you purchase will often be longer than those required, particularly if you can cut two or three pieces to size from one plank or beam. It is always worth doing a little arithmetic in order to minimise waste.

A charming circular pond with statuary.

An informal rock pool in a Japanese garden.

A moulded fibreglass pond is camouflaged with plants.

An informal pond planted to look perfectly natural.

CONSTRUCTION METHODS

The materials chosen to construct your water feature will determine the construction methods used. If you do not have the necessary skills, you may want to hire an artisan to assist you, or even employ a contractor to do the work. Always ask for references and check with previous clients before deciding to use outside services.

Setting out

Before you do anything else, it is necessary to mark out the position of your water feature. Whether you are building a raised pool or sinking a pond into the ground, peg out the area, or outline its proposed position with a hose-pipe, rope or chalk.

The simplest pond to set out is an irregular one which is to be sealed either with a flexible liner, concrete, clay or bentonite. Here accuracy is not essential, providing you maintain the basic size and shape you have used for estimating materials.

When utilising a rigid shell, you can place this on the ground and draw around its perimeter. If it has a symmetrical shape, place it upside down so the lip is included in the layout; otherwise stand it upright and simply allow for any wider areas.

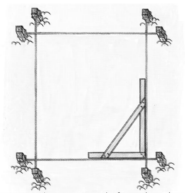

A home-made square made from three lengths of wood in the ratio 3:4:5 is useful for setting out rectangular and square pools.

For a rectangular or square pool, it is essential that corners are at right-angles. A reliable way of doing this is to use what is known as the 3:4:5 method. A home-made wooden square (*see* illustration) is helpful here, especially if the pond is small; or you can use a steel builder's square and a tape to check for accuracy. First of all, the two diagonals must be identical when measured from corner to corner. Check this and then, working from one corner, measure 300 mm (1 ft) and 400 mm (1 ft 3¾ in) along the two adjoining outside edges. Mark these points with pegs and check the distance between the two pegs. It should be 500 mm (1 ft 7¾ in). Repeat at the other three corners.

Aluminium silicate and soil are mixed thoroughly during the sealing process (clay puddling).

To set out a circular design, you can use a 'compass' made with pegs and string. Simply knock a peg or stake into the centre of the proposed pool area and attach a piece of string to it, the length of the radius. Attach the end to a second peg or stick, pull the string taut and scrape it around in a circle to mark the circumference on the ground.

An oval shape is marked in a similar way to a circle. Two stakes are driven into the ground and a piece of string is attached to them to form a loop (*see* illustration). Pull the string taut and stick a peg in the ground at the furthest point. Repeat several times around the perimeter, so indicating the basic outline. Note that the closer the pegs are to one another, the more circular the shape will be.

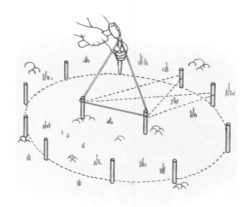

A circle is marked out with a single peg and string, but for an oval shape, it is necessary to use pegs and a loop of string. Use additional pegs to demarcate the shape.

Sealing with sodium clay

The technique used to seal a pond with sodium clay or bentonite powder is similar to the traditional method of clay puddling. Whichever material you use, it is vital to compact it thoroughly to make the pond basin thoroughly impervious.

Sealing with bentonite is a relatively simple operation, but as with any other building method, it is important to follow the correct procedure and to use materials mixed in the correct proportions.

Excavation is the first step, but since the bentonite is mixed with soil, some of this must be retained on site. This special clay may be used to waterproof any shape or size pond. However, it is essential that the walls do not slope more than 1:3. If the gradient is too steep, it will be impossible to compact and seal the sides.

It is vital to remove all stones and vegetation and smooth out the soil so you have an even surface. If rocks are to be retained in the design, it is best to reposition these once compaction is complete.

You will need to compact the interior of the shell before the bentonite is spread over the surface. A homemade punner (*see* page 10) is adequate for most small ponds; or you can use a mechanical compactor, provided it is suitable for use on the sloping walls.

The quantities of bentonite required for pond sealing are specified on page 18. It can either be laid as a blanket over the pond basin, or mixed in with the soil. If applying a mixed blanket, you can blend the soil and sealant first, perhaps using a concrete mixer; or you can mix the two materials on the pond floor.

When sealing ponds with a pure blanket of bentonite, it is absolutely essential that the material is spread out evenly. It is only compacted after it has been covered with a 300 mm (1 ft) protective layer of soil and the entire area moistened slightly. Always ensure that the whole operation is completed the same day.

If you decide to mix the bentonite with soil, the simplest method is to spread it over the surface, cover this layer with about 100 mm (4 in) of soil, and mix it together thoroughly *in situ*. If you blend the materials externally, it is important to establish exactly how much soil you need.

This layer must be thoroughly hydrated prior to compaction. Then spread another 100 mm (4 in) layer of soil on top, water lightly and compact some more.

Whichever method is used, it takes a while for the water to react with the bentonite, but when it does, you will see the top layer of soil drying out. After about 48 hours, wet it again; leave overnight and fill the pond the next day.

Where fibrous matting impregnated with bentonite is used, this is laid over the floor and sides of the pond and covered with compacted soil.

Installing liners

No building skills are necessary to install liners in the ground, although it is vital to ensure that the upper edges of the pond are level. If one side is higher than the other, this will be obvious once the pool is full. A spirit level set on a straightedge will enable you to check the surface around most ponds. A post set absolutely vertically in the excavation will enable you to pivot the straightedge and so check levels at different points around the perimeter; a method which is particularly useful for a circular or oval shape. If the pond is very large, you may have to use a dumpy level (*see* page 11).

Flexible liners are particularly simple to fit. Regardless of which material you are using, the liner is draped into the hole so that the centre sags on the ground. The edges are secured with bricks or stones around the perimeter and the pond filled with water.

As you fill the pond, you can straighten out some of the creases and folds. The success you have will depend on the material you are using. Butyl rubber is probably the most flexible liner available; and PVC tends to stretch into the excavated shape more easily than polyethylene.

It is not necessary to trim the liner to the shape of the pond until it is full. Trimming is done with sharp, multi-purpose scissors,

A pre-cast fibrecement pond installed in a sloping garden has been cleverly camouflaged.

leaving 300-500 mm (1 ft-1 ft 8 in) around the edge. Tuck the edge of the liner into the soil and place rocks or slabs around the edge; or secure by paving over the excess liner as illustrated on page 51.

Some people advocate lining the excavated hole with a layer of soft sand before installing the flexible liner. This step is only really imperative on a stony site; usually any twigs, stones and other sharp objects which could damage the liner once it is filled with water, should be removed before the liner is fitted.

Rigid liners may be installed both below and above the ground, but you will have to build a supporting wall of some sort around a raised pond.

Concrete was used to build this dual-purpose pool which may also be used for swimming.

For below-ground ponds, installation for all types of rigid liner is basically the same as for the project on pages 48-49. It is necessary to dig a hole slightly larger than the shell and ensure that the base of the excavation is flat and smooth. Use a spirit level and a straightedge, and ensure that you bed the shell so the lip is below the surrounding ground, otherwise you will not be able to hide the rim with an edging.

Once the liner is in position, shovel sand or soil between the walls of the shell and the sides of the hole. It is a good idea to bed the liner on a layer of well compacted sand. If the design you choose includes a plant shelf, the excavation must allow for this. Care should be taken to backfill and compact thoroughly so that it is stable.

A raised pond should be set on a flat, level surface before the space between the liner and the wall is backfilled to maximise rigidity and stability.

While some people backfill with mortar or a dry cement and sand mixture, the high alkalinity of cement may, over a period of time, lead to the deterioration of materials like fibreglass.

Working with concrete

Concrete pools may be hand-packed or made by pouring the mixture between shuttering. Whichever method is chosen, there are certain basic principles which should always be followed regarding the mixing, laying and curing of concrete.

If you are building a large pond with concrete, it is advisable to consult an engineer for advice regarding the stresses that the pressure of water will create.

Batching is essential for mixing concrete in the correct ratio. For DIY projects, the simplest and most effective way to batch materials is by volume, using the same size container for each component. Fill the vessel flush with the rim and, if possible, use a whole sack of cement for each batch.

When employing unskilled labourers, make sure that the correct ratios are used. A common mistake is the assumption that 1 bag of cement mixed with three, four or six wheelbarrow loads of sand is a 1:3, 1:4 or 1:6 mix. This is wrong, since a builder's wheelbarrow can hold about two 50 kg (110 lb) pockets of cement and you will end up with a mixture which is far too weak for pool construction. If you are using a waterproofing additive, follow the manufacturer's instructions carefully.

Mixing concrete takes effort rather than skill. For small projects, it is common to mix by hand, in which case you will need a clean, hard surface, or a wheelbarrow. Never mix directly on the ground as water will be absorbed from the concrete and soil will contaminate it; and do not be tempted to mix on existing paving as it is very difficult to clean.

Start by mixing a batch of sand and cement together and then form a hollow in the centre. It is not necessary to measure the water; use a garden hose to pour it into the centre very slowly, shovelling and turning the dry materials as you do so. It is best to add water bit by bit, scooping the mixture from the outside to the centre, until it is soft and workable, but not runny. Add the stone last, with more water if the concrete mix is too dry.

If you decide to use a concrete mixer, the above procedure is reversed, with the stone and a little water being added first to prevent the mortar clogging the blades. Then add the sand and cement with more water to obtain the correct consistency.

Bitumen products are often used to seal concrete ponds.

A man-made water feature incorporates cascades and pools. Various water-loving plants, including Cyperus papyrus *give it a natural charm.*

Placing concrete in foundations directly against the ground, can result in some loss of moisture. To minimise this, dampen the soil in the foundation trench first, and allow the water to soak in before laying the concrete.

Once it has been placed, the concrete must be well compacted or vibrated to get rid of all air bubbles. With a straightedge or wooden beam, use a chopping action to compact and a sawing motion to level. Finally, check the surface with a spirit level to ensure it is absolutely flat.

When handpacking concrete to form an irregularly shaped pond, it is best to use a slightly drier mix and to angle the sides slightly outwards to prevent the mixture from sliding to the base. You should use some sort of reinforcing to hold the mixture in place and strengthen the shell. Weld mesh (or even galvanized chicken wire) is commonly used to line the excavation, ideally with spacer blocks made from cast mortar or timber, set between the soil and the mesh to help ensure that the reinforcing stays in the centre of the concrete so that the shell is evenly strengthened. Most reinforcing mesh comes in a roll and you will have to cut it with a hacksaw and bend where necessary to fit the shape.

While the framework of a hand-packed swimming pool should be about 150 mm (6 in) thick, 80 mm (3 in) is adequate for

Shuttering enables concrete to be cast in situ.

most ponds. In cold climates, where frost is a problem, thicker shells with extra reinforcing are recommended.

To ensure the finished edges of the pool will be at the same level on all sides, mark a constant height with pegs around the perimeter before you start the concrete-work (*see* page 42). Use a water level to check their height.

The procedure of handpacking concrete is basically the same as throwing a foundation, although you cannot use a straightedge for compacting and levelling the material. In this instance, it is best to use a round trowel, stamping the concrete to expel the air and level the surface with a float to smooth it off (*see* pages 54-55). Remove the pegs before the concrete sets and smooth over the holes.

Shuttering is sometimes used in the construction of formal pools with vertical concrete walls. This is an especially useful method on a sloping site, or where a raised pond is required. It is also essential for the construction of concrete bridges.

A delightful little brick pond incorporates a circular planter around its perimeter.

The first step is to cast a slab (*see* Foundations, below) or, in the case of a bridge, strip foundations on either side of the water. Once this has set, construct a strong, rigid formwork using timber boarding braced with wooden battens. The shape of the formwork, or shuttering, will determine the configuration of your structure. Since the formwork must be removed after the concrete has set, it is sensible to oil it lightly before pouring the mixture.

Position the reinforcing prior to erecting the shuttering, and only remove the shuttering after approximately 14 days, when the concrete is well set.

Curing is necessary for concrete to gain its maximum strength. Since it is the water which starts a chemical reaction causing the cement to harden, it is essential that sufficient moisture remains present in the newly cast material. It is important that the temperature of the concrete does not fall below 10 deg C (50 °F). To aid curing, the concrete should be sprayed now and then with water; and in cold weather, it should be covered with sacking or black polyethelene to insulate it.

It takes about 28 days for the concrete to gain most of its strength; but, provided there is some moisture present, it will continue to strengthen for several years. It is important to realise that concrete does not get strong by drying out. In fact, if it is allowed to dry out too quickly, it can crack or even crumble.

Since 'ponding' water on the surface of newly-laid concrete will actually help it to cure, you can quite safely fill a pond after about 48 hours.

Finishes for the concrete shell range from render or plaster to waterproof bitumen. If these are disregarded, there is a good chance your pool will leak, even if you have used a waterproofing additive in the concrete mixture. At the very least, a slurry of cement and building sand should be rubbed over the surface. The koi pond featured on pages 54-55 was rendered and then coated with a rubberised bitumen sealer. Other waterproofing possibilities are mentioned on page 17.

Another factor to consider is that the inherent lime content of the cement, can be harmful to plants, fish and animal life. If you do not coat the internal surface with some kind of sealant, you will have to drain the water from the shell once or twice to rid it of any impurities. Each time you fill the pond, leave the water to stand for a couple of days so that it absorbs the lime residue. A commercially-available chemical lime neutraliser can also be used.

Bricklaying and stonework

Even though bricklaying skills are not essential for the creation of ponds, raised structures built from brick or stone look particularly attractive, especially if they are formal in style.

Foundations are essential for all ponds and pools constructed with bricks, blocks or stone. While the required dimensions will vary depending on the height of the wall and other factors, a depth of between 100 mm and 200 mm (4-8 in) is ample. It is normally a good idea to cast a slab foundation which acts as the base of the pond as well as the support for walls.

The weakest spot in a pool built this way will be the point at which the floor joins the walls. As a safeguard, especially in deeper ponds, it is prudent to set reinforcing in the concrete and to build this into the brickwork.

Laying bricks is not particularly difficult, but it is vital to recognise the importance of the basic principles of square, level and plumb. A brick structure that does not stand upright and is not level, will look odd, and is likely to leak.

The tools required to ensure your structure has a really professional finish are all detailed on pages 10-12, and the method of setting out a pond is described on pages 20-22.

The next step is to practise using a trowel, since this important tool is used throughout the bricklaying process. You will need it to spread the mortar, to butter the bricks and bed them firmly into place, and to scrape off excess mortar.

Once the foundation has set, mix the sand and cement together with water in exactly the same way as for concrete (*see* page 18), but without adding the coarse aggregate. The mixture should be reasonably thick and porridgy, and pliable enough to work with.

Lay mortar in a strip along the foundation where the brick wall is to be positioned, and use your trowel to create an uneven furrow down the centre. Since the first course of bricks is the most important of all, it helps to string a builder's line to check that it is straight. A steel builder's square can also be used.

Begin bedding the bricks in the mortar, ensuring you have an even 7-10 mm (¼ in) joint between each. You can fill the joints after bedding the bricks, but it is easier to butter one end of each brick as you go. Do this by lifting a blob of mortar with the trowel and squashing it onto the short side of the brick. Slide the brick into position and then tap firmly with the handle of the trowel, to bed and level it.

Before starting on the second course, it is essential to check that the bricks you have already laid are level (*see* page 10). From this point, corner blocks and a line may be used to keep each successive course straight; and a gauge rod, to ensure that mortar joints are even (*see* pages 11 and 12). A spirit level should be used frequently to check both horizontal and vertical brick surfaces.

Another critically important building principle to remember is bonding. If the load of the bricks is not properly distributed, even a low wall can collapse. There are various different bonding patterns.

The most common type is stretcher bond, a pattern formed with each brick overlapping the one below by half.

As the brickwork progresses, use the trowel to scrape away excess mortar. This is especially important when using reconstituted stone or facebricks, although it will still be necessary to use a pointing tool or piece of metal to neaten the joints when building is complete.

Stonework is similar in many ways to brickwork. However, while brick courses are even, stone may be laid randomly or in courses with a regular horizontal joint and irregular vertical joint (cut stone).

A dry stone wall, built without any mortar, is obviously only suitable if it is designed to camouflage a rigid shell set above the ground. More commonly, stone is bedded in mortar, and the same tools used for checking levels and corners.

To simplify the task of waterproofing, it makes sense to aim for as even an internal surface as possible. For this reason, cut (or dressed) stone is an obvious option, even though it is not widely available. Unless you have the special equipment and necessary experience, it is usually best to employ the services of a stonemason or artisan with stone-cutting skills.

Rendering is a useful skill for pond builders to acquire, as a variety of brick structures are finished this way. The internal shell of concrete and stone pools may be rendered with a cement/sand mix.

The mortar mix – which can be exactly the same as that used for bricklaying – should preferably contain plasticiser to make the material more pliable and therefore easier to spread over the surface.

It is applied to the brickwork or concrete shell with a rectangular or rounded trowel and pressed down so that it will adhere. The trowel is then used to scrape it flat before it is smoothed with a wooden float. In hot weather, it helps to splash a little water on the render as you work. Finally, corner trowels are used to neaten edges and both internal and external corners.

External plaster or render must be kept damp in exactly the same way as concrete, to ensure it cures and does not crack.

It may, however, be painted with a rubberised bitumen within a relatively short period of time.

Tiling and paving

Two of the most obvious options for a pool or pond surround are tiles or paving. The basic principles involved are much the same for all these related materials, although the preparatory work does vary from project to project.

Tiles must always be laid on a solid base, and you will therefore first have to throw a concrete slab. If you are going to bed them with a cement-based tile adhesive, you will have to screed the surface with mortar. Some tiles, including the terracotta type, may be laid on a bed of mortar set directly on the concrete.

After approximately 72 hours, once the screed has set hard, mix the tile adhesive according to the manufacturer's instructions. This product is spread with a notched trowel which forms ridges to aid adhesion, and the tiles are then pressed firmly into place.

A formal fountain mounted on a plastered wall features fish and a gargoyle.

An attractive pre-cast concrete fountain.

A formal brick pond with planters.

A steel square and a straightedge will enable you to lay tiles at the required angle, and spacers (made of plastic or metal) will guarantee equal joints. Use either a line or a length of string to mark the edge and secure each end under loose tiles or bricks. A rubber mallet is the best tool to tap the tiles so that they are level. Simulated stone designs and some handmade quarry tiles are slightly uneven in thickness; use a spirit level to check that the upper surface is flat. If any of the tiles are lower than the others, lift and spread a little extra adhesive on the base of the unit.

Laying tiles on an adhesive layer is generally less messy than laying them on a bed of mortar. However, in both cases, these materials should be wiped off before they dry and stain the surface.

Grouting is done after about 48 hours, when the adhesive is dry or the mortar has set. Use ready-mixed grout or mix the powdered type with water, according to the manufacturer's instructions, and spread thickly over the joints. All the excess should be wiped off immediately with a sponge, especially if you are using very porous tiles.

Tiles that have been laid on mortar can be grouted with a 1:3 cement and sand mixture. When mixed with water, it should be fairly dry and crumbly. A small pointing trowel may then be used to fill and smooth the gaps. Any mortar staining the tiles should be wiped off immediately.

Paving may be laid on concrete, but it is more usual to lay bricks, blocks and slabs on sand. Not only is the second option quicker, but it is also cheaper.

If the ground is unstable, you will need to excavate 100–200 mm (4 in–8 in) to accommodate a sub-base of crushed stone or gravel before spreading the sand. This should, in turn, be thoroughly compacted, by hand or machine.

When laying any form of paving directly on the existing ground surface, remove all vegetation before compacting. The layer of sand should be no more than 30 mm compacted to 25 mm (about 1 in), and it should never be used to level uneven ground. Smooth it with a straightedge before you start laying the bricks, allowing a slight slope for drainage (see page 29).

Pavers may be laid in a number of patterns, and the joints filled with sand or a weak mortar mix. A steel square, spirit level and builder's line will assist in producing a professional finish. A rubber mallet is useful for tapping the pavers into place.

The recommended cement:sand mix for jointing clay bricks laid on sand is 1:6, while a slightly stronger 1:4 mix should be used when jointing pavers, flagstones and setts made from concrete, or clay bricks which have been laid on a concrete base. Either brush the material in dry and afterwards spray the surface lightly with water; or alternatively, use a trowel to fill the gaps with a crumbly mix.

Cutting tiles and bricks can be a wasteful business; however, it is one of those inevitable tasks which must be tackled. Using a bolster and brick hammer is relatively simple, once you get the knack. Place the brick on the ground, preferably on a thin bed of sand, and then use the chisel end of the bolster to score the surface on all sides. Position the bolster on the cutting line you have made and tap the handle end firmly to break the brick. Another method is to score a cutting line with the chisel end of a brick hammer, and then continue tapping around this line until the brick breaks.

When tiling, special cutting machines which score and break the tile are useful, and certainly more efficient than using a manual scribe and nippers. Thick quarry and terracotta tiles should be cut with an angle grinder using the appropriate disc.

Edging and coping

The principles involved when laying any kind of edging are dependent largely on the materials used; and this, in turn, will depend primarily on the type and style of pond or pool you have built. For instance, grass may be allowed to grow right up to a clay-puddled pond, but it is inadvisable as an edging for a liner pond where any erosion of the bank could be disastrous. Tiles or brick paving look beautifully sophisticated laid around a formal, symmetrical pool, while rocks, stone slabs and even timber will be more appropriate if used to edge a natural pond. A coping will only be necessary around raised pools, to finish off the supporting wall.

Edging around any water feature will be one of the final tasks of any project. There are various options and, except for raised decking erected alongside the water, it is important for all types of edging and surround to be laid on a soil bed that is sound and well compacted.

A simple fish-pond, designed for koi, and set in a sheltered Oriental-style garden, has a characteristic stone edging around its perimeter.

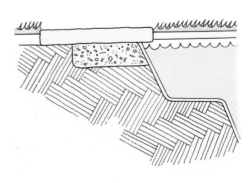

Lay paving slabs on a concrete foundation to prevent the edges of the pond from collapsing.

Grass has been allowed to grow to the edge of this natural pond, constructed to encourage wildlife to visit the garden.

Although not always necessary, a collar of concrete laid around the perimeter of the feature will stabilise the edging. Where bricks are used as an edging around pools they should be securely set in mortar to ensure they do not come loose.

Slabs, bricks and even tiles may be laid to overlap the edge of the water slightly. This hides the shell and, in the case of polyethylene and PVC, protects it to a certain extent. By sloping these away from the water very slightly, excess water and mud can be prevented from washing into the pond in rainy weather.

When laying the edging, a common problem is that excess mortar falls into the pond. Not only is this messy, but lime in the cement damages plants and can kill fish. For this reason, it is essential to clean the shell before filling the pond. If it is already full of water (which will be the case if you have fitted a flexible liner), then drain and clean it before introducing any type of pond life.

Coping will finish off any raised pond or pool. Various materials are suitable, including paving bricks, tiles and simulated stone slabs. Either match the coping to the wall – topping a facebrick structure with matching paving bricks, or use a contrasting material – perhaps tiles on a rendered wall, and timber atop dressed stone.

Most materials will be cemented into place, although it may be necessary to bolt timber to stabilise it. The upper surface of stepping stones may be finished in exactly the same way.

Woodwork

Only the most basic carpentry skills are needed for the average water garden project. Provided one knows how to use the necessary tools – drills, saws and so on – simple decks, jetties and even bridges may be tackled by enthusiastic amateurs.

You will, of course, need to know how to cut and join timbers competently, and which connectors to use to secure them.

There is no need for elaborate joints in garden structures, and most of the time you can rely on the simplest arrangement which may be nailed, screwed or bolted.

Cutting timber across the grain is the normal procedure for this type of woodwork. This may be done with a tenon saw, handheld power saw or a circular bench saw, which is what most professionals would use. You will need to secure the timber to get a clean cut, preferably by clamping it to a workbench. You will usually saw the ends of beams, railings and so on perfectly square; when you mitre corners, however, it will be necessary to make an angled cut.

Joints, as already mentioned, are essentially simple. The main intention is to keep them neat, safe and secure.

Even a reasonably large deck can be built with ordinary butt joints (where two pieces of wood are joined without any fancy cutting), some of which may overlap

Rudimentary carpentry skills were all that was required to fashion this effective fountain feature made from well-sealed railway sleepers.

Wood screws are the most common choice for carpentry and it is important to choose the right one for the job. Coach screws, which have a hexagonal head and are tightened with a spanner, are particularly useful for garden structures. Most screws are partially unthreaded, but self-tapping screws have the thread right up to the head, giving a better grip. They may be fixed with a screwdriver or a drill, and are often used to secure decking slats and handrails for bridges. Self-tapping screws can be screwed directly into softer woods, but to prevent the wood from splitting, it is best to drill a pilot hole, thinner than the screw itself, before you begin.

Where timber is attached to masonry or brickwork, special expansion bolts (called Rawl bolts) are invaluable. Hexagonal bolts, which, like coach screws, are tightened with a spanner, and cuphead or coach bolts, may be used to affix heavy beams and upright timbers used for decking and pergola structures.

Nails are easily hammered into timber, but they sometimes pull out easily. In general, longer, thicker nails will be more secure than short, thin ones, although you must take care not to split the wood. Ideally, a nail should be more than double the thickness of the wood you are fixing. To strengthen the join, first glue the two pieces of timber. Dovetailing the nails, by hammering them in at an angle, will help prevent the wood from twisting. While wire nails are used for rough carpentry, ring shanked nails have a good grip and may be used when fitting decking slats.

When nailing very hard woods, it helps to drill a small pilot hole first; and when nailing soft timber, it is best to blunt the tips of the nails slightly to prevent the wood splitting.

The cheapest nails and screws are made of steel, but this material will rust unless it has been anodised, galvanized or coated in some other way. Where ordinary steel is used, it is best to countersink screws just below the surface and fill up to surface level with a filler. Nail heads can be hidden by prising up a sliver of wood before hammering the nail into place, and then gluing the bit of wood back in place.

Finishes applied to timber are as varied as the wood itself. Wood should be treated with a preservative and it is usually necessary to protect it from excessive weathering by oiling, varnishing or painting.

The most common choices are specially formulated wood dressings and water-repellent finishes that soak into the wood, and various tinted varnishes which add a depth of colour to the structure.

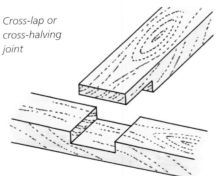

Cross-lap or cross-halving joint

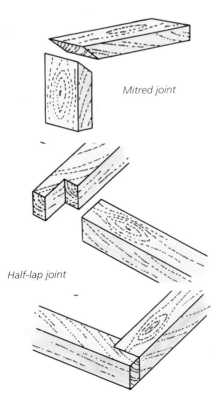

Mitred joint

Half-lap joint

to form a T- or cross-lap joint, and other elementary connections. These include lapped joints, used to lengthen pieces of timber, and half-lap joints where two pieces of wood are cut out so that they slot together snugly to form a beautifully flush surface. Both half-lap and mitred joints may be used to create neat corners (*see* illustrations).

Securing the connections is quite elementary, and a variety of nails, screws and bolts may be used. The secret is knowing which item to use where.

An unusual water feature flows across the brick-paved driveway.

FINISHING OFF

Once your water feature is complete, you may connect the electrics, fit the pump and perhaps a filter, and make sure you are happy with the lighting arrangements in this part of your garden or patio. Plants and fish may now be introduced to ponds, pools and the surrounding areas. It is sensible to make sure you have paid attention to drainage around the water feature and are familiar with the steps that must be taken to maintain it properly.

Drainage

Wherever there is water, drainage is an inevitable factor. In most instances, solutions to any potential problems can be easily found.

Unfortunately, a disadvantage of a water garden established where water occurs naturally is that you are likely to have muddy, boggy areas around the pond, at least when it is rainy. In fact, if any pool overflows during wet weather, this will inevitably result in mud and slush.

A solid edging and adjacent paving will minimise potential problems. The surface should slope away from the pond very slightly, to allow for water run-off. Where an adjacent patio abuts the house, the paving must always slope away from the building. The finished surface should be at least 150 mm (6 in) below the damp-proof course (DPC) of the house, or below the internal floor level.

If grass is grown right up to the water, you may be faced with erosion of the bank. While this is not a problem with bentonite or clay ponds, which seal themselves, mud will slide into a rigid shell and flexible liners may start to collapse.

One solution is to establish a bog garden around the perimeter of the pond (*see* pages 58-59), but access to the water will be limited. Alternatively, you can dig a trench around the water's edge and fill it with stones or gravel to create a French drain and conceal it with plants.

Drainage holes are seldom included in ponds nowadays; and they should, in any case, be avoided. Even though a plughole can be well sealed with silicone, this will always be a particularly weak point which could result in leakages. Besides, unless the draining water is led right away from the pond by underground pipework, the water will inevitably erode beneath the structure and probably cause it to collapse.

Another problem is excess water which overflows in rainy weather. In severe instances, the sides and banks of a pond tend to erode and fish may be swept out of the pond.

In high rainfall areas, it is sometimes advisable to install an overflow system of some sort to cope with all the excess water. The simplest is a pipe or channel which leads to a gulley, French drain, or even a bog garden.

A severe drop in the water level is also damaging. Not only can it affect fish and plants, but if you have used a polyethylene liner, prolonged exposure to sunlight will cause rapid deterioration. If bentonite was used, the exposed surface may crack unless the water level is raised.

If the level drops, either top-up the pond with a hose-pipe, or install an automatic top-up system to maintain a constant water level. The most common method is to use a ball valve similar to those found in toilet cisterns. Set to the correct level, it

A drainage channel filled with stones or gravel helps prevent mud collapsing into a turf-lined pond.

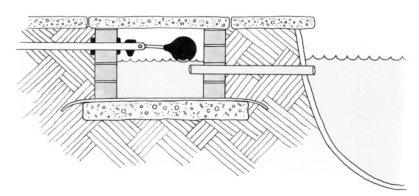

An automatic top-up system keeps the water level of the pond constant. Use a piece of PVC pipe to link the reservoir to the pond and a ball-valve to regulate the flow of water from the mains supply.

automatically allows water fed through a pipe from the mains to fill up the pond. You may want to hide the ball itself under a wooden platform or beneath a fake GRC or fibreglass rock. Alternatively, the ball valve can be set in a small reservoir tank next to the pool, and perhaps camouflaged with a paving slab (*see* illustration below). This operates rather like the cistern itself, feeding the water to the pond through a connecting pipe.

There are sometimes restrictions regarding the connection of pools to the mains water supply, so check with your local authority first.

Pumps and filters

Water and electricity do not mix, and new installations as well as modifications to existing wiring, should be overseen by an electrician. It is just as important to check the official regulations which are applicable to electricity in the gardens in your area. In some countries only low-voltage supplies may be used near water and a transformer may be required.

Where the pump is connected to a household electrical circuit, you will usually be protected by an existing circuit breaker (or trip switch). However, it may be necessary to install one of these units on a separate circuit to detect deviations or leakage in outdoor current .

Many of the electrical appliances and fittings available for use in and around water features can be safely and effortlessly installed without taking extra precautions or seeking professional assistance. Electric cables are easily protected in conduiting

A selection of pumps, fountain accessories and adjustable-flow fountain heads (right). Transparent flexible and black semi-rigid tubing are also pictured.

(or armoured cable), which can then be buried in the ground. Specially designed weatherproof boxes will enable you to plug in submersible pumps outdoors and to operate fountains and waterfalls at the touch of a switch.

If you are not sure of your own capabilities, consult a qualified electrician.

Pumps are essential for the recirculation of water, so if you decide to install a fountain, waterfall or cascade, this will be an important piece of equipment.

There are two main types of pump – submerged or housed on the surface. Your choice will depend largely on the volume of water involved. While a small pump will be adequate for most fountains, you will obviously require a more powerful unit for a large water feature incorporating waterfalls and flowing streams.

The pump output (described in litres or gallons per hour) will be specified on the packaging, and the dealer will usually be able to advise which pump is best for your particular needs. Take care not to choose one that is too powerful, as excessive turbulence churns up sand and dirt in the pond, making the water murky. When installing a fountain, it is important to ensure that the water head is compatible with your design – the water head (*see* page 94) being the distance between the maximum fountain height and the pond water level. The pump should be capable of spurting water to the required height.

Submersible pumps are generally simple to install and operate, and an added advantage is that they do not have to be primed. Most have a strainer on the inlet to prevent fish or floating debris from being sucked into the moving parts.

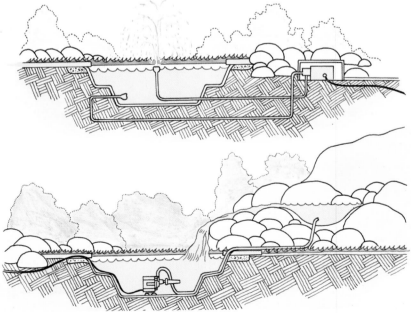

Both surface pumps (top) and submersible pumps (bottom) may be used to recirculate water and operate fountains.

Fountain jets (featured on page 66) are often fitted directly to submersible pumps and some are sold with interchangeable jet fittings. Quality is varied, but the more expensive ones generally have an adjustable flow.

A submersible pump can be used to operate a fountain in a large pond, but do consider accessibility. If the strainer requires cleaning, you should not have to wade into the water. Instead, be sure to site the pump near the edge of the pond, on a ledge or loose-laid bricks, and run a pipe to the jet in the centre.

These units are completely sealed and attached to a cable which can be plugged into an appropriate waterproof box. This box is, in turn, connected to the internal electrical system. Conduits and cables can even be run from the pump directly into the house and plugged into an internal wall socket. In very cold climates, where freezing temperatures are experienced, the pump should be removed from the water in winter.

Surface pumps, including those used for swimming pools, are expensive and sometimes noisy, but they are usually the only option for larger water features.

The siting of these pumps is important; they should be located near the pond, preferably just below the level of the water and housed off the ground in a waterproof box. Alternatively, you could cover the unit with a fake, hollow rock.

Some surface pumps have to be primed manually, but self-priming models are available. If a pump will not prime, or if it loses its prime while running, check whether there are any leaks in the pipes leading to the pump, whether the impeller is broken or the pump seal is faulty. The pump operates by drawing water from the pond through a strainer and suction pipe – these could be blocked or the water level in the pond may have dropped.

A certain amount of plumbing is inevitable with any pump and it is important to use non-toxic fittings. Plastic is usually the safest option.

Filters, like pumps, may be housed outside the pond or submerged in the water. Generally though, the external type is preferred as these are more reliable and much easier to keep clean.

Just as swimming pool filters are used with a pump, so too are pond filters. A major difference though, is that swimming pool filters rely on chemicals for effective sterilization of the water, thus making it safe for human use. A pond filter is used to keep the water clear and to rid it of harmful waste materials including dead

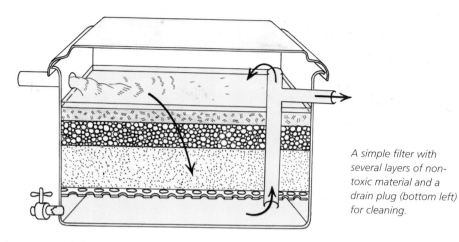

A simple filter with several layers of non-toxic material and a drain plug (bottom left) for cleaning.

plant matter, fish excreta and uneaten fish food. A relatively simple mechanical filter will sieve out dirt, waste and algae and it can be run sporadically as needed. A biological filter allows natural organisms to flourish in its confines, helping to break down decaying plant material as well as the waste excreted by fish.

The simplest biological filter is a box (sometimes made of fibreglass) which contains various filter media. The more advanced varieties consist of several chambers with valves, and make use of the usual filtration material.

The size of the filter you will need always depends on the volume of water in your pond and the number of fish it contains.

If the filter does not have the required capacity, it will not keep the water clean. When installing the filter, follow the manufacturer's recommendations regarding the flow rate. If it is too high or too low, the filter will not operate efficiently.

A new filter will take several weeks to mature and it is best to wait a while before introducing fish (particularly koi). Once it is running, the filter should only be disconnected when it is necessary to clean it. This type of maintenance does not take long, but should be done at regular intervals to prevent a build-up of waste. Use pond water rather than tap water which will damage the biological organisms essential to the efficient working of the filter.

A hollow fake rock has been used to hide the filter.

Adjustable spotlights illuminate an elaborate moving water feature at night.

Concealed lighting effectively highlights this attractive water feature.

Lighting

Lighting relies on electricity and is subject to the same concerns as pumps, but there is no doubt that water gardens benefit from illumination. Effective garden lighting improves security and safety, enhancing water features after dark and improving surrounding areas.

Methods of lighting various objects and areas in the garden range from direct illumination, which casts a spot or single beam, to a selection of decorative uplighters and assorted lamps.

When deciding how to light your outdoor area, it is wise to consider function. For instance, general lighting is best reserved for patios, and floodlights for tennis courts and driveways. Paths, steps, decks, bridges and so on should be lit with safety in mind. Visitors need to see where they are walking and confusing shadows from partly-concealed decorative lighting can make these areas hazardous. It is essential that fittings are positioned in such a way to avoid light shining directly into people's eyes.

It is best to combine several types of lighting, perhaps making use of free-standing lamps for walkways, spotlights to add interest to plants, and uplighters to highlight a waterfall or cascade. Another option is to make use of underwater lighting from within the pond, for example, to emphasise a fountain (*see page 67*). Special submersible lights are, of course, necessary for this purpose.

Fittings chosen for gardens in general, and water features in particular, must be manufactured for outdoor use. A sealed unit which can be exposed to all weather conditions is essential. While this sounds limiting, there is a wide range available, from wall-mounted carriage lamps to spots attached to stakes which may be anchored in the ground.

Whatever you choose, make sure the fitting is in keeping with the style of your garden. There is little point in achieving a beautiful effect at night, if the light looks ugly during the day. Run-of-the-mill units should be hidden beneath foliage or behind rocks.

Long-burning candles can be very effective around water features. Candles also look charming when floated on the surface of a pool.

Installation should usually be carried out by a professional, although there are DIY kits (or similar fittings) which can be easily positioned without any help at all. Most include spotlights on spikes for sticking in garden beds. Like many pumps, the whole system is plugged into a waterproof box linked to the existing electrics. Proper outdoor cable should be used. This should preferably be threaded through conduiting before being buried in the ground. Wherever two lengths of flex are joined, the connection must be protected with a waterproof coupling.

Lighting which is near or attached to the house will usually be part of the internal electrical arrangement. These lights are simpler to install than new fittings in the garden, which have to be on a separate circuit. If this is the case, an external circuit breaker may have to be installed.

Planting

Water features are part of the garden scheme as a whole. As you will already have a good idea of the effect you are aiming to achieve, this will influence your choice of plants.

An informal pond will benefit from a combination of luxuriant planting around the edges, plant life on marginal shelves and aquatics in the pool itself. Planting around the perimeter is also a good way to camouflage any exposed concrete or liner. If yours is a formal raised pool surrounded by brick paving, you will be limited to floating and aquatic plants and possibly plants in pots.

Plants grown around the pond and in beds adjacent to it, should blend in with the surrounding garden. You are certainly not limited to bog plants or marginals, but these will often look most attractive. Some examples include the fernlike *Astilbe* species, marsh marigolds (*Caltha* species), irises and *Mimulus ringens* (monkey flower) as well as arum lilies (*Zantedeschia* spp.), which are surprisingly hardy, even if cultivated in cold climates.

Avoid shrubs and flowers that will look out of place, even if the soil allows you to plant them. Roses will look quite odd around a wildlife pond, whereas *Gunnera* species, ferns and various grasses will look natural. Roses may, however, be planted around a formal fountain.

Bog plants love moisture and will grow quite happily on the banks of informal ponds. Alternatively, you can establish a bog garden where they will flourish (*see* pages 58-59). Unlike marginals, most plants in this group should not have their roots permanently submerged in water.

Various lilies, including *Zantedeschia* (arums), the *Hosta* species (plantain lilies), *Hemerocallis aurantiaca* (day lily) and South African *Schizostylis coccinea* are ideal bog plants, as are a wide range of ferns. *Lobelia cardinalis*, most of the *Primula* species and *Trollius* species (globe flowers) will also thrive in these conditions.

Marginal plants, as their name suggests, grow in the shallow water along the banks of ponds and pools. The construction of marginal shelves ensures their inclusion in the planting plan, although some may be grown in pots set on loose bricks or flat-topped stones. Although partly submerged, these plants do not play a role in maintaining a balance of life in the pond. Instead they are decorative, providing colour and softening the water's edge.

Planting marginals directly in the shallows of some ponds is possible, but it is more common to grow them in baskets or pots. These can be removed when it becomes necessary to divide the plant. It is best to allow one container for each plant and to group them together. Never plant different varieties in one pot.

A combination of water-loving plants thrive in and around the pond.

There are many suitable marginal plants, ranging from rushes and grasses (some of which can be quite invasive), to water mint (*Mentha aquatica*) and various flowers. To introduce colour to a pool, certain water buttercup types like *Ranunculus flammula* (lesser spearwort) or *R. lingua grandiflora* (greater spearwort) are ideal. *Pontederia cordata* (pickerel weed) and other flowering aquatics like irises (available in numerous colours) will also add touches of brightness.

Oxygenators, which are submerged aquatic plants, are essential for the balance of life in any pond. They help keep the water clear and provide both food and a place for fish to spawn. Usually sold in bunches, these 'water weeds' are useful for getting rid of algae, as they absorb the minerals and carbon dioxide on which algae thrive. They should not be dropped into the water, but rather weighted down in soil or gravel at the base of the pond.

Oxygenators are usually available from suppliers of pond fish.

Floating aquatic plants are usually introduced to ponds where surface cover is required. There are not many suitable species in this category, as many are invasive. Most duckweed varieties, for instance, can multiply at an alarming rate and should be controlled. Try to find star duckweed (*Lemna trisulca*) as this is the least invasive specie. Water hyacinth (*Eichhornia crassipes*) can be a menace in warm climates, but it is popular in Britain.

One of the most distinctive floating plants is *Pistia stratiotes* (water lettuce), with its rosette-like leaves and feathery roots. Although it is easily killed by frost it will survive cold weather.

The full range of plants suited to pond life.

Deep-water aquatics have submerged roots and stems, but their leaves and flowers float on the surface. They adequately replace water lilies in small ponds where fountains constantly disturb the water.

There is not a great variety of plants in this category, and the water hawthorn (*Aponogeton distachyos*) and the water fringe (*Nymphoides*), with its pretty yellow flowers are probably the best known. They should generally be planted to a depth of at least 300 mm (1 ft).

Water lilies are in a class of their own and they certainly take pride of place in any pool or pond. There are various types, some of which are more hardy than others. Not only are their flowers decorative, but water lilies also shade the surface of the water and help to keep it clear.

They love full sun, but will not thrive in moving water and should be grown well away from fountains or waterfalls. The recommended planting depth varies from 100 mm–1 m (4 in–3 ft) depending on the particular variety.

Water lettuce (Pistia) *is an attractive aquatic plant which can become invasive in hot climates.*

A natural pond will soon attract frogs.

Keeping fish
One of the primary reasons for building a pond is to keep fish. They bring life to the water and add colour and interest.

There are numerous fishes to choose from, ranging from the common goldfish to ornamental koi. Your choice will depend on the amount of money you wish to spend and the amount of time you have to take care of them. Goldfish and other inexpensive pond fish will generally take care of themselves, while costly koi require more attention.

Bear in mind that koi, undoubtedly the most impressive of all pond fish, must be kept in aerated and filtered water. This not only enables you to see them more clearly, but it is also essential for their health.

Goldfish living in an established pond will get all their food from their environment. Supplementary feeding of koi is much more important. Koi will often eat right out of your hand; but do not let this encourage you to overfeed them.

Having decided what to buy, it is important not to overstock the pond. It is vital that fish have sufficient oxygen and space to grow. When in doubt, seek advice from your supplier.

When introducing the fish into the pond, float the water-filled bag in which it was bought, on the surface for about an hour to prevent a sudden temperature change. Then open the bag carefully and let the fish slip in and swim away. Empty the water into the pond.

Maintenance and repairs
Maintenance of the majority of water features is minimal. There are certain tasks, however, which will ensure their appeal all year round. For safety reasons, these chores should definitely include regular scrubbing of any accessible surfaces which might become slippery. In addition, if you have installed a filter and/or a pump (*see* page 30), these will have to be cared for and regularly serviced. Any repairs to the shell or surround of the pool should be undertaken as soon as possible, to prevent further deterioration.

Maintenance
Upkeep of your water feature is essential, and with a regular programme you will be able to avert problems and prevent a pond from becoming an unkempt quagmire or simply a breeding ground for mosquitoes.

Water In most ponds, the water simply has to be topped up from time to time as some degree of evaporation is inevitable. Do not allow the level of the water to fall more than about 50 mm (2 in) below the average, or plants, fish and plastic liners could be damaged. Bentonite ponds will tend to crack.

Decomposed water lilies and other aquatics sometimes cause an oily film to develop on the water. This can usually be removed by pulling a sheet of newspaper across the surface. If, for some reason the water becomes badly polluted, you will probably have to remove any fish and drain the pond.

Unless you filter the water in a fish-pond, dead organisms and waste products from the fish will eventually build up and become toxic. To avoid this happening, change the water partially once a year, in spring or autumn.

Green, murky water is usually caused by algae, which grows rapidly if the surface of the water is constantly exposed to sunlight. Algae will not harm the fish, but its growth should be inhibited to clear the water and ensure a good balance of life within the pond. The simplest way to do this is to shade the surface with floating plants and water lilies which have beautiful leaves or pads. If this does not work, you can introduce a chemical algicide or fit a filter. Some people advocate placing a bag of straw on the bottom of the pond; this absorbs the algae and other impurities, but it must be replaced periodically.

While the degree of alkalinity or acidity (the pH) of swimming pool water should be maintained between 7.6 and 7.2, water in a fish pond may range from 8.5 to 6.5. A simple test kit may be used to measure the pH of the water from time to time. A high pH may be caused by excessive lime in the water or a build up of green algae. If it rises above 9.0, it is too alkaline. Both fish and plants will suffer unless it is rectified with suitable chemicals. Acid water with a pH below 6.0 is unusual – an adjacent peatbog or accumulated organic acids from decomposing fish waste could be the cause.

To empty a pond, insert a length of hose or some other flexible pipe into the water and suck on the other end to create a vacuum. The only prerequisite is that the open end of the hosepipe should be lower than the pond. If it is not, you will have to use a pump to drain it.

Plants Seldom a problem in the water garden, plants do not have to be watered, and many types thrive to such an extent, that all you have to do is thin them out from time to time and remove the sections that are no longer required.

Apart from controlling pond weeds and floaters, dead plants and fallen leaves should be removed from the pond – decaying organic matter produces gases which are toxic to fish. This can be fatal, especially in areas where ice forming over the pond surface in winter prevents the gases from escaping. If a layer of ice does form, a hole should be made so the fish are not harmed. Check it regularly to ensure it does not ice up again.

There are certain pests and diseases which affect aquatic plants, and it is best to remove the affected foliage and stalks and to hose down the remaining plants.

Slippery surfaces One of the most dangerous aspects of a pond is slippery surfaces. Moss and algae will quickly gain a foothold where constant moisture is present. Check surrounds, stepping stones, wooden steps, bridges, and so on from time to time. Scour and scrub them with clean water to make sure that they are slip-free.

Repairs
Fixing minor problems may be necessary at times. If the water level of your pond drops suddenly or you find that the edges of surrounding paving are loose and unstable, major repairs may be required. You may have to empty the shell before the necessary repairs can be undertaken.

Do not be tempted to simply top up the level of the pond daily. This results in the surrounding soil area becoming very marshy and the entire structure could be severely undermined.

Ornamental koi are colourful and characterful.

Liners All liners are problematic once they have been damaged. Some rigid liners do tend to crack after a few years and you may even find it necessary to replace the entire shell. As flexible sheeting can deteriorate in the sunlight, it too will have to be replaced if this occurs.

PVC and polyethylene sheeting may be punctured by sharp objects, but you can repair both types of plastic quite successfully. Special vinyl repair kits are available. You could cut your own patch from a piece of the same type of sheeting and glue it over the hole or tear. Unfortunately, few adhesives are satisfactory, and it is best to experiment before trying to mend the sheeting. When using a repair kit, be sure to follow the manufacturer's instructions carefully. Surprisingly, a well-known clear adhesive, patented in England and manufactured for use on china, plastic and leather, works well on PVC. You do not even have to drain the pond as it sets very quickly underwater. It will also adhere to polyethylene underwater but only for a limited period. This means that you may need to replace the patch periodically.

Concrete Ponds that are constructed from concrete sometimes develop leaks, especially if they have not been rendered and coated with a waterproof sealant. The most common reasons for leaks are incorrect concrete mixtures made with too much (or the wrong type of) sand and the subsidence of foundations. Tiny fractures can be sealed quite efficiently with bitumen. Distinct cracks should first be chipped out and filled with mortar or a proprietary patching plaster. Do not be tempted to use an ordinary filling compound as this will be too porous. If the crack opens up again (or if you cannot find the leak), it is best to line the pond with a flexible material or, better still, to seal it with fibreglass.

Timber If wood starts to deteriorate, replace it immediately. Not only will this avoid expensive structural repairs to your water feature at a later stage, but if the timbers split or rot, the entire structure could become dangerous.

The water lettuce (Pistia) in this pond is contained in a floating netted frame to prevent koi from nibbling its feathery rots.

PONDS AND POOLS

Most ponds and pools are permanent features which are constructed using rocks, bricks, concrete and other materials. These structures can be set in the ground, raised above the level of the surrounding garden or patio, and have either a formal or informal appearance. Even a prefabricated pond or a pool made with a flexible liner will usually be fixed into position permanently, and should therefore be carefully placed to achieve the effect you desire.

The many methods of pool and pond construction have been discussed on pages 13-17, and the importance of siting the pool wisely mentioned on page 9. You will have to decide what suits your needs.

While few gardens ever prove totally unsuitable for any kind of water garden, the size of your pond may be limited by the proportions and conditions of your property. Before you start digging holes and spending money on materials, make sure that you can accommodate the pond of your choice satisfactorily.

Having decided that you want your own pond, the initial question will be what to build and where to locate it. While a well-constructed, thoughtfully planted and properly cared for water garden will undoubtedly provide many hours of pleasure, a badly positioned or neglected pond can be a disaster.

If it is not correctly installed and adequately maintained, or sufficient attention given to the balance of life within the pool, the water may become stagnant and unsightly. Worse still, the murky, green water will soon become a home for unwelcome midges and mosquitoes.

An informal koi pond incorporates simple decking and a timber walkway over the water.

FUNCTION

It may seem strange to consider the function of pools and ponds, but you will soon realize how important this is. The requirements of a person wanting a formal, raised pond as the central feature of an entrance courtyard, will be quite different to those of somebody who plans to stock expensive Japanese koi. Similarly, the approach taken when constructing a face-brick pool for goldfish will be unlike that undertaken when establishing a duck pond or even a lily pond.

It is important to consider your priorities at the planning stage. Do you want a reflective pond? Is it more important for you to hear the sound of trickling water?

Do you want to incorporate a rockery, waterfall or fountain into the plan?

Both water plants and fish add an exciting dimension to ponds, but plants and fish have varying needs. It is best to avoid rapid moving water if you aim to have a beautiful display of water lilies. You will need to provide a ledge or shallow end if you are planning to introduce decorative marginal plants like irises, arum lilies or bulrushes. If you intend to keep fish, decide now on which type you want. While the demands of ordinary goldfish are minimal, the requirements for keeping exotic koi are quite specific. For the latter,

your pond will have to be deep enough and the water capacity sufficient for the number and size of fish you are going to stock. You will also need aerated water and a filter to keep the water clear (see pages 31 and 34). The introduction of koi to your pond will limit your water plants, as these fish are notorious nibblers of certain plant varieties.

DESIGN

When designing a pool or pond, it is essential to decide from the outset on the effect you wish to achieve. This will depend largely on whether you are aiming for a formal feature or natural pond. Whatever you choose, ensure that it fits the style and proportions of your house and garden. If yours is an established property, you may have to compromise and settle for a design that conforms with the existing character of your garden. When starting from scratch, it might be necessary to enlist the help of a professional landscaper or landscape architect.

The size of the pond itself is an obvious factor and one which relates directly to the possible sites available. If space is limited, you will inevitably be forced to build a small pool. Many small pools and ponds are charming and effective, but if you are extremely pushed for space, you may decide on a more elaborate, but contained feature (see pages 88-93).

Where size is not a factor, you will find that proportions will be largely governed by the function you have identified for your pond. Ducks need enough water to swim in, and, as already stated, koi require deeper ponds than goldfish. For a reflective pool to be effective, it should have a reasonably large surface area. A decorative formal pool, built for the sake of introducing the sound of water may be as big or small as you wish, depending of course, on its location. A tiny pond set in a vast open area will tend to be overlooked. Instead strive for a sensible balance.

Apart from the pool itself, good design will incorporate the area around the pond as well. This relates not only to rocks, waterfalls and plants, but also to the pool surround and adjacent paved areas. In fact, the edging chosen will often determine how well the entire water feature blends with its environment.

If you plan to spend time near the pond, or to create an entertainment area adjacent to it, make sure you have plenty of room around the water's edge. Do not overlook the decorative details – when siting a pool against a wall, consider the addition of a spouting gargoyle or cement fish (see pages 44-46). A raised courtyard pool could be improved by placing a precast fountain of some sort in the centre.

LOCATION

Having decided what type of pond or pool you want, you will have to select a site for it. A formal raised pool will always look good in a courtyard or perhaps on a patio. A natural water garden needs to be established where it will blend harmoniously with its surroundings. This type of garden should be accessible and visible, especially if you plan to keep koi. There is little satisfaction in spending time establishing a concealed feature which you cannot

This impressive DIY bentonite pond features an island and an attractive waterfall.

Stepping stones invite one to cross this unusual water feature.

enjoy. Furthermore, if your pond is hidden away at the bottom of the garden, it is an invitation for neglect. Perhaps the only exceptions are the ponds located in a 'secret garden' where you escape for solitude, and those that are planned specifically to attract birdlife.

Although it is not a good idea to choose an exposed site for your pond, it is best to avoid overhanging trees, especially if they are deciduous. Decomposing leaves encourage the growth of green algae and produce salts and gases which could be harmful to fish and other animal life.

The encroaching roots of some trees can also be problematic and could damage some of the less robust liners (plastic sheeting, for instance).

Choose a site that is sheltered from the wind by nearby evergreen trees and shrubs, or construct a screen that will provide some protection. Reeds, bulrushes and even some large shrubs and trees, can provide welcome shade for part of the day. Alternatively, you could consider incorporating some sort of overhead shelter like a pergola. Located alongside a pond, this will provide some protection

A simple duck pond in the country has an inviting air of tranquillity which invites one to linger just a little bit longer.

from the sun for those wanting to sit and enjoy the view. Another popular option is to situate ponds and pools close to the house, where they can be seen and appreciated, even on rainy days.

A vital factor when choosing the best site are the services linked to your house. Any underground cables, water mains, sewerage pipes and so on must all be located prior to excavation and construction. If you are building a pool above the ground, these may not be a problem, but it is still sensible to identify any possible obstacles in the planning stages.

First, ascertain where your power source will be if you are planning to incorporate fountains, waterfalls, or install a filter or electric lighting. It may be necessary to incorporate underground conduiting (*see* pages 30-31).

In the event of unstable soil conditions or a high water table, it is usually more sensible to choose an above-ground design. If the water table is high enough to make construction difficult, you may be able to build up the sides of a rocky pond and incorporate a bog garden alongside it.

Unlike a swimming pool, which is reasonably deep, ponds may be relatively shallow, a factor which should simplify excavation. Unless yours is to be an expansive water garden or pool built in a rocky outcrop, you will probably find you can dig by hand. In the event of needing earth-moving equipment to excavate, it is vital to ensure the site is accessible for bulldozers and other similar machinery.

Proof that even an ordinary pre-cast pond can be installed so that it looks like a natural rock pool.

FORMAL PONDS AND POOLS

The two basic garden types are defined as formal and informal. Ponds and pools are classified in the same way. There is a tendency to refer to the formal version as a pool and the informal as a pond, which is not strictly correct. Some garden experts prefer to relate *ponds* with a living element (fish, water lilies, and so on); referring to *pools* when only water is involved.

Since ponds and pools are defined in the dictionary as small, or fairly small bodies of still water, we have tended to use the two words interchangeably. Nevertheless, the idea of a formal pool conjures up an aura of sophistication; straight, symmetrical lines or classical curves and circles set within a large paved area or structured garden planted in the same style.

Somehow a formal pond seems less rigid. Whatever its shape and whichever definition you prefer, formal ponds and pools will be clearly defined and often geometrical. They may be raised, sunken so that one steps down onto the edging, or set at ground level. They are at their best on a formal patio or in a courtyard, where a wall may be used as a backdrop.

As there is always the danger that the area alongside any area of water will become muddy and marshy, it is sensible to edge a formal pond. To create a more effective frame, pave or cover a generous

Dramatic reflections in a lily pond.

area around it. Plants in pots can then be introduced if you feel the area looks too stark. The containers should be symmetrically placed and matching. It is best to use one type of plant for effect.

Whenever a hard surface is incorporated in the plan, the material used should fit the formality, as well as complement the existing surfaces in your garden. Tiles, brick paving and marble (for those who can afford it) are all good choices. This does not mean that you cannot use ordinary, inexpensive materials if you wish. Even pre-cast slabs can be very effective if they are laid to match the symmetry of the

feature. It is best to avoid mixing materials or planting right to the edge of this type of pond, as this will give the area a less formal look. There is nothing to stop you from planting grass, but it must be kept well mown or the effect will be spoilt.

The decision to build a formal pool or pond is often related to function. You may wish to continue the theme established by carefully balanced planting. An informal garden, with gentle curves and irregular flower beds, will not provide a satisfactory venue for this more severe style.

Although a large lake (however irregular its shape) will have reflective qualities, most reflective pools are formal in style. If this is your choice, it is important to establish what will be reflected in the water. Apart from light (which includes romantic moonlight), it will reflect changing colours and shapes; not only of trees, shrubs and flowers, but of nearby buildings and any other structures. If these are unsightly, you may decide to plant a screen of quick-growing bushes to camouflage them.

Pots or statuary alongside the water, or a fountain set within it can be very effective provided the container or ornamentation chosen is in keeping with the style.

A lily pond constructed in this style can be impressive; and there is nothing to stop you from keeping fish in a formal pool.

The idea of reflected images is heightened by two symmetrical formal ponds placed in line with one another.

FORMAL FACEBRICK POND

A formal, reflective pond need not necessarily be large. Provided a portion of the water surface is kept clear of plantlife, even the smallest pond can have dramatic, reflective qualities. This design, which was built with just 150 bricks in a single weekend, is raised above the ground and is deep enough for both fish and aquatic plants.

By restricting plantlife to water lilies and potted papyrus (*Cyperus papyrus*), a good expanse of water is still visible. The inside surface of this pond was painted with four coats of rubberised bitumen sealer to make it watertight. You may, if you wish, render the walls as well as the concrete floor before sealing to help guarantee it is impervious and will not leak (*see* page 25). Other waterproofing possibilities are mentioned on page 17.

STEP 2

STEP 3

Materials
For a rectangular pond,
   1.9 m x 1.2 m
   (6 ft 4 in x 4 ft):
125 facebricks
25 paving bricks
175 kg (385 lb) cement
435 kg (0.4 cu yds) sand
250 kg (550 lb) stone
waterproofing additive (optional)
20 litres (4½ gal) rubberised bitumen
   sealer (depending on brand)

An old tractor tyre, without its inner ring, painted and used as a sandpit, provides a place for children to play, but does little to enhance the appearance of the garden.

Preparation
1. Peg out the area of the pond and string a line between the pegs. Then dig out the soil to about 300-400 mm (1 ft-1 ft 4 in).

Concrete
2. Now for the arduous part. Mix the concrete in the recommended ratio 1:2:2 (cement:sand:stone) and roughly line the bottom and sides of your excavated hole, levelling the concrete mixture with a spade or trowel. For this pond, you will need almost two bags of cement for your concrete. If you wish, you can add a bonding compound (waterproofing additive) to the mixture to improve the waterproof qualities of the pond, but follow the manufacturer's instructions carefully.

STEP 1

3. Use a trowel to get the surface reasonably smooth (*see* page 12), taking care to level the upper rim which will form a foundation for your low brick walls. Leave the concrete to set for at least 24 hours before tackling the brickwork.

Brickwork
4. Lay out the first course of bricks to ensure they fit and then mix mortar in the ratio 1:3 (cement:sand) as mentioned on page 18. You will need approximately three-quarters of a bag of cement (37.5 kg or 82 lb 8 oz) to lay all the bricks, but only mix as much mortar as you can use in two hours.

5. Now you can begin laying the bricks in the usual way (*see* page 24). Remember to check frequently with a spirit level to ensure that they are level and plumb. Use a builder's square to make certain all four corners of the pond are at right angles.

6. Corner blocks and a line will help you to keep the brickwork straight and level. Since you are laying light-toned facebricks, it is important to clean off all excess mortar as you work. Scrape the trowel upwards against the brick to do this.

7. Continue to build up the walls until you have five courses, then top this with paving bricks to finish it off neatly. You could also use tiles, or larger paving slabs which would overlap the wall slightly.

STEP 6

STEP 10

8. To achieve a really good, even finish, use a piece of metal or a jointing tool to rake out a little of the mortar between the bricks. Allow the mortar to set overnight.

Sealing

9. It is essential that the concrete base of the pond is rendered. To ensure the pond is watertight, you may render the inside walls, but you will have to increase the quantities of materials listed. Ensure that the render is about 15 mm (½ in) thick.

10. Once the render has set, you can paint on the rubberised bitumen sealer, polyurethane or any other suitable sealant. Follow the manufacturer's instructions and thin the first coat if required.

Filling the pond

11. When the bitumen is dry the pond can be filled with water. You can add interest to the pond by placing river rocks on the bottom and grouping plants around them. If necessary, set pots on bricks or flat-topped rocks to achieve a good balance of plant life in the pond (*see* pages 32-33 for ideas on appropriate plant species).

The completed pond has been incorporated into a paved patio where grass would not grow. Additional plants around the adjacent tree trunk add to the lush and now tranquil surroundings.

POND WITH PLANTERS

Imaginative design and creative thinking will enable you to build more elaborate formal ponds which incorporate planters and fountain features. This enchanting formal koi pond combines the benefits of a reflective water surface with the sight and sound of water. The ingenious fountain spillway was custom-made from glass. The design includes four planters, one of which accommodates a submersible pump. A biological filter is housed above the height of the fountain, behind the back wall, to allow the water to flow out automatically, with gravity. The front section of the pond is deeper than the back section to provide for the needs of the exotic koi. Quantities given presume you are building against an existing wall. If not, you will need more bricks, cement, sand and stone.

Materials
For a pond with measurements as shown in the illustration:
862 facebricks
850 kg (1 875 lb) cement
1.45 m³ (1.9 cu yd) sand
0.6 m³ (0.7 cu yd) stone
waterproofing additive (optional)
15 l (3¼ gal) rubberised bitumen sealer (depending on brand)
3 m x 40 mm (10 ft x 1½ in) semi-rigid tubing
2 elbow connectors
1 x submersible pump, with 5.5 m (18 ft) water head (pumps 70 l or 15 gal per minute)
1 x biological filter with 4 400 l (968 gal) capacity
1 x 350 mm x 700 mm x 10 mm (1 ft 2 in x 2 ft 4 in x ⅜ in) sheet fibrecement (or similar material)
1 x 700 mm x 160 mm x 10 mm (27½ in x 6¼ in x ⅜ in) glass or perspex
1 x 700 mm x 60 mm x 10 mm (27½ in x 2¼ in x ⅜ in) glass or perspex
3 x 80 mm x 40 mm x 10 mm (3¼ in x 1½ in x ⅜ in) glass or perspex, with one end splayed to 50 mm (2 in)
silicone sealer

Preparation
1. Peg out the pond according to the dimensions shown in figure 1, but allowing an additional 100 mm (4 in) on all sides for the foundations. Then excavate to a depth of about 350 mm (1 ft 2 in). You will have to dig out an additional 650 mm (2 ft 2 in) of soil from the front rectangle which is deeper.

Concrete
2. You will need 8 bags of cement for the concrete, which should be mixed in the ratio 1:2:2 (cement:sand:stone), with a waterproofing additive if you wish. Throw a strip foundation for the walls of the planters, and for a dividing wall between the two sections of the pond (see area indicated by dotted lines in figure 1). Note that the dividing wall extends from the base of the lower pond to the base of the upper one.

3. You should throw slab foundations for both ponds and the small planter which will contain the pump. First build the dividing wall as described on page 24. Allow time for the mortar to set and then fill any remaining gaps behind the wall with soil and compact well.

4. Now you can throw the slab foundations using a straightedge to level and compact the concrete as described on page 23. Use a spirit level to check your surface, then allow the foundations to set for at least 24 hours. Note that there is no concrete on the base of the three additional planters.

Brickwork
5. Since this is a fairly complex design, it really will help to lay out the first course of bricks without mortar before you start laying. You will need about 300 kg (660 lb) cement for the mortar which should be mixed in the ratio 1:3 (cement:sand).

6. Lay the bricks in the usual way (see pages 24-25), in stretcher bond, remembering to use the correct levelling tools

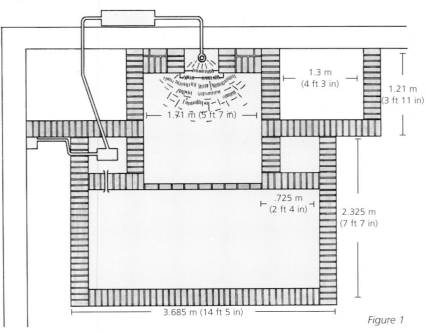

1.3 m (4 ft 3 in)

1.21 m (3 ft 11 in)

1.71 m (5 ft 7 in)

.725 m (2 ft 4 in)

2.325 m (7 ft 7 in)

3.685 m (14 ft 5 in)

Figure 1

(*see* page 10). The procedure is the same as that followed for the previous project, but there are more corners and so additional checking will be necessary to ensure that the structure is properly built. The front section of the pond comprises brick walls which are eight courses high (excluding the coping), with only a single course above ground. The back planters are nine courses high, with six extending above ground level, while the two small planters are only four courses high. Leave a couple of unmortared gaps in the wall between the main pool and pump compartment for the free flow of water. Also leave a small gap to accommodate the pipework which leads to the filter.

7. Lay the bricks on edge as a header course so forming a coping on top of the walls. Note that this particular design incorporates a double course of coping bricks on the inner wall of the small planters (*see* figure 1).

8. Rake out the joints and allow the mortar to set.

Fountain
9. Lay the bricks for the fountain feature according to figure 2 below. Two piers, approximately 650 mm (1 ft 2 in) apart and measuring 540 mm x 340 mm (1 ft 9 in x 1 ft 2 in) are built up six courses in stretcher bond (*see* Laying bricks, page 24).

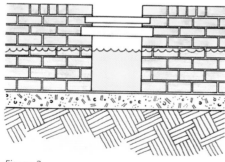

Figure 2

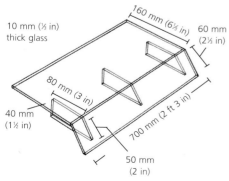

Figure 3

An unusual formal koi pond with planters and an intriguing spillway fountain adds life and interest to a brick paved patio.

10. Place the sheet of fibrecement over the gap between the two piers and build up a further two courses, with a half-brick course spanning the opening to create a weir. The height of the finished fountain construction is slightly lower than the surrounding planter walls.

11. Make up the fountain spillway by gluing the five sheets of glass or perspex together with a clear silicone sealer (*see* figure 3). When the structure is thoroughly dry, lay it across the front of the opening and then lay the coping as indicated in figure 1.

Pipework and wiring
12. Knock two holes in the wall behind the pond so that you can lead the pipework from the filter to the fountain and the pump. Push one end through the hole you previously left in the one small planter. Do not connect the pipe to the pump until the interior surface has been rendered and sealed with bitumen.

13. To enable you to lead the power cable unobtrusively from the pump, drill a hole in the side wall of the same small planter.

Plaster or render
14. The floor of the pond, including the planter which will house the pump, and the internal walls may now be rendered. Mix 150 kg (330 lb) cement with 0.3 m³ (10 cu feet) of sand and add sufficient water to make the mixture pliable. Include a waterproofing additive and plasticiser in the mix if you wish.

15. Working from the back wall, lay on the plaster or render with a plasterer's trowel, applying pressure to make it stick to the bricks. Work in sections, smoothing with a plasterer's float once it has settled, and using corner trowels to neaten the corners. Note that the render here is about 20 mm (¾ in) thick.

16. At the same time, render in the pipework where it enters and exits the various walls.

Sealing
17. Allow the smoothed render to set for at least 24-48 hours before painting on a rubberised bitumen sealer or any other suitable sealant, according to the manufacturer's instructions.

Pump and filter
18. The bitumen does not take long to dry, and then you can place the pump in its own compartment and connect it to the loose pipe. Connect the other end of the pipe to the filter, which should be positioned above the fountain spillway.

19. Remove the electric plug from the pump and take the power cable through the hole previously drilled. Replace the plug and connect it to an external socket in a waterproof box. Seal around the cable with silicone sealer.

Finishing off
20. When the sealant is completely dry, you can fill the pond with water and plant the additional structures.

FEATURE POOL

This attractive water feature, which combines a small pool and fountain, was constructed alongside a courtyard wall. It makes use of a small recess and has been rendered (plastered) and painted to match the existing wall. It measures less than one square metre (10 sq ft) in area, but the pool is 440 mm (nearly 18 in) deep and quite adequate for goldfish and floating plants. Not everybody will have a garden wall with alcoves, so materials specified for this project presume that you will be building against one which is straight. If these dimensions do not suit your site, it is quite simple to adapt the plan to make it larger. While it is not essential to include the wall-mounted fountain, this does add an element of movement to the feature and introduces soothing sounds to the area.

Materials
For a 1.2 m x 900 mm (4 ft x 3 ft) pool:
48 bricks
80 kg (176 lb) cement
200 kg (2 cu yd) sand
95 kg (210 lb) stone
waterproofing additive (optional)
3-4 l (½-¾ gal) rubberised bitumen
   sealer (depending on brand)
pre-cast gargoyle
1 x M6 x 50 mm (2 in) Rawl bolt
1 x 800 mm x 12 mm
   (2 ft 8 in x ½ in) tubing
2 x 100 mm x 12 mm
   (4 in x ½ in) tubing
2 x elbow connectors
1 x submersible pump, with 1.4 m
   (4 ft 6 in) water head
outdoor cable and conduit
silicone sealer

Preparation
1. Peg out the proposed area with the two short sides of the rectangle at right angles to an existing wall.

2. Remove any existing hard surface from the site (in this particular case, paving bricks were removed) or dig out approximately 100 mm (4 in) of soil to form a foundation trench.

A dilapidated, old tub, planted with a variety of herbs is overgrown, unkempt and on the brink of becoming unsightly.

3. Now level the foundation trench and compact it thoroughly with a punner (*see* page 10).

Concrete
4. Mix concrete in the ratio 1:2:2 (cement:sand:stone), with about 45 kg (100 lb) of the cement, taking care to add only enough water for a workable consistency (*see* page 18). Place the mixture in the trench and distribute it evenly over the area with a spade. Here the concrete is spread so that it is level with the upper surface of the adjacent paving.

STEP 5

5. Using a slight chopping motion, now compact the concrete with a short plank and then use a plasterer's float or trowel to smooth the surface. Allow the foundation to set overnight.

Brickwork
6. Using a 1:3 ratio of cement to sand (with about 16 kg or 35 lb of cement and 50 kg or 100 lb of sand), mix the mortar with water to the correct consistency. String a builder's line or use the adjacent paving as a guide and spread a sausage of the mixture on top of the edges of the foundation. Bed your first brick in the mortar and tap it firmly into place with a trowel. In some cases, you may have to deviate from a straightforward plan. Here, one wall of the pond extends from a step, so several paving bricks have been removed, and one section of the wall built on the elevated concrete base of the step.

STEP 6

7. Continue laying along the three open edges of your foundation. Use a spirit level to ensure that the brickwork is absolutely level and a builder's square to check that all the corners are at 90°. Corner blocks and a line will also help you to keep the brickwork straight.

8. In order for the construction to bond adequately, it will be necessary to cut some of the bricks. You can do this with a brick hammer or a chisel (*see* page 12).

STEP 7

STEP 8

9. As the wall progresses, you must continue to check both vertical and horizontal planes with a spirit level. If the pond is not square, level and plumb, it will look odd and your efforts will have been wasted.

STEP 9

STEP 10

STEP 11

Preparation for the fountain

10. If you have decided to install a fountain, you can measure and mark its position as soon as the mortar used to construct the wall is dry. In this instance, the outlet is to be located at a central point in the recess, about 900 mm (3 ft) above the pond floor. The pencilled 'X' indicates the position of the outlet. Remember that the height of the gargoyle or other fixture must be compatible with the water head of the pump used.

11. Referring to the mark you have made as a guide, chase a channel into the wall. Do this by cutting two parallel grooves down the length of the wall with an angle grinder, and then chipping out the render between them with a cold chisel. Make sure that the channel is deep enough to accommodate the pipework and render which will conceal it. For the 12 mm (½ in) tubing used here, you will need to create a course at least 20 mm (¾ in) deep.

12. Measure the distance between the outlet and the hook on the back of your gargoyle or panel, and mark this point on the wall above the outlet. Using a masonry drill bit, bore a 6 mm (¼ in) diameter hole long enough to accommodate your 50 mm- (2 in-) long Rawl bolt. Slot it into the hole and tighten the nut.

13. This pond, constructed in a courtyard, is not sited against a boundary wall, therefore the cable from the submersible pump can be routed through the garden wall and channelled into the house. Alternatively, you can direct it through the side wall of the pond, or run the cable over the edge of the structure (*see* page 73). If you are drilling through the wall, use a masonry drill bit long enough to penetrate the thickness of the structure. Also make sure that the size of the hole is just large enough for the cable. If it is too big, you will more than likely have a problem sealing around it.

STEP 13

14. Run the cable to an outside weather-proof box connected to your electricity supply (*see* page 31).

15. Before you start the plasterwork, attach an elbow connector to each end of the 800 mm (3 ft 8 in) length of tubing.

Plaster or render

16. Now render the pond using the remainder of the cement and sand mixture, plus a waterproofing agent (waterproofing additive) if you wish. Mix these materials with water as described on page 22. Start by first rendering the tubing into the channel in the back wall. Once it is in place, only a section of each elbow connector will be visible.

STEP 16

17. Taking care not to dislodge the pipework, trowel the render onto the foundation floor and both internal and external walls of the pond, ensuring the finished covering is about 15 mm (just over ½ in) thick. Try not to get any of the render mixture in the hole you have drilled for the electricity cable.

18. Once the walls and floor are well covered with render, use a wooden float (*see* page 12) to smooth the surface. Then neaten the edges of the pond with a corner trowel.

Installing the fountain

19. After making sure that the render is completely dry, carefully push the two small pieces of tubing onto the exposed ends of the elbow connectors. One end of the tubing will be connected to the pump outlet and the other will slot through the mouth of your chosen fountain feature.

20. Now mark the height of your proposed water level and paint the bare render above it. Do not paint the inside of the pond.

21. When the paint is dry, slide the gargoyle (or, in this case, fish panel) into position so that the tubing fits through the mouth and the panel hangs securely on the bolt. Trim any protruding tubing with a sharp utility knife.

Sealing

22. Unless you are running the power cable over the edge of the pond, you will have to remove the plug so that you can insert the cord through the hole previously drilled in the wall. Position the pump below the gargoyle to ensure you have enough cable in the pond and then use a suitable silicone product to seal the points where it enters and exits the wall.

23. Finally paint on several coats of rubberised bitumen or an alternative waterproof sealant up to the proposed water level, following the manufacturer's instructions.

Operating the fountain

24. Once you have filled the pond with water you will be able to plug in the pump, switch on the electricity and enjoy the fruits of your labour. Plants in pots will enhance the area if placed symmetrically. Use only one type of plant to complement the formal style of this pool.

The completed pond adds sophistication to the courtyard. The addition of a wall-mounted fountain introduces sound and movement.

STEP 17

STEP 19

STEP 23

INFORMAL PONDS AND POOLS

Unless the architectural genre of your house fits a formal garden style, it is likely that you will plant the garden in an informal manner. Even if your house *is* formal in style, you may still decide on a more casual or natural approach outdoors.

Informal gardens are typified by gentle curves and flowerbeds of irregular form; and the water gardens which accompany them may have the same kind of design. Straight lines and geometric shapes are out, symmetry is forgotten and rigid planting is frowned upon.

Although some people build informal ponds in the centre of lawns, this often looks contrived. You will achieve a more authentic effect if you blend it in with the surrounding environment. It is essential to hide the material from which the pond has been constructed.

Bog plants and decorative marginals may be planted around the edge of the pool, overhanging the water here and there, effectively blurring the outline you have created. You can also place rocks and river stones along the edge and in the shallows.

If you have a natural pond in your garden, you will probably find it is sited at the lowest point. It may also be fed by a natural stream. It stands to reason, therefore, that a man-made pool of this sort should be similarly located – ideally in a spot which looks as though it could be a natural pond. Avoid hollows which will quickly fill with mud. If an adjacent slope is likely

Water trickles into a lily pond.

to erode and wash soil into the water, stabilise it with interlocking concrete terrace blocks which you can plant, or establish a rockery (*see* page 54).

Sloping ground also offers the opportunity to create natural waterfalls and cascades, with a series of ponds on different, terraced levels. This will take more expertise, and it might be necessary to get the help of a landscaper.

If your aim is primarily to attract wildlife to the pond or even simply to create a natural water feature which blends with your garden, there is no doubt that you will want an informal design. Whatever the size of the pond you are planning, the key to success on flat ground lies largely in the peripheral planting and edging chosen. One of the most successful ways to make

it look natural is to plant right to the water's edge. The only problem is that, for full enjoyment, you need to see the water. A raised platform or patio on higher ground will give you visual access, but you may find it difficult to get there through the growth. Here, a jetty, adjoining deck or a natural clearing are the obvious answers. You could grass an adjacent area, or pave it. If a hard surface is your choice, consider materials which look natural; crazy paving or reconstituted stone, for instance.

Although a timber edging of railway sleepers or cut logs can look beautifully natural, it is a good idea to intersperse the wood with ground cover or pebbles to prevent it becoming too slippery.

Pay careful attention to what you plant both in and out of the water to ensure a healthy balance of life. Equally important are the kinds of fish you introduce into the pond and the wildlife you attract to the area. Water lilies and floaters provide shelter, while various aquatic plants oxygenate the water. These plants also provide a haven for insects, frogs and many other creatures which inhabit water gardens.

Unfortunately, fish fall prey to many birds and this can be a problem, especially if you have invested lots of money in a koi pond. In some instances, the answer is to cover the pond with a suitable net. While this may detract from the general effect, if you can remove it at will, it may prove be a satisfactory solution.

River stones line a catchment pool which cascades downhill into a man-made duck pond.

PRE-CAST POND

This type of pond is undoubtedly the simplest and most foolproof of all, as the pre-cast shell guarantees instant results. The designs available and materials used to manufacture the shell will differ in various areas, but the principles involved in sinking one of these ponds remain the same. Since most are manufactured in irregular shapes, pre-cast shells are commonly used to create informal ponds.
The secret of making them appear natural is to disguise obviously man-made finishes, and to hide the edges. The pre-cast fibrecement pond featured here has a kidney shape and is approximately 270 mm (10½ in) deep, with a flat, level base. The reconstituted stone paving slabs, which look less contrived than most other materials, cover an area of 1.2 m² (13 sq ft).

STEP 3

Materials
For a 1.1 m x 1.8 m (3 ft 7 in x 6 ft) pond:
1.75 m² (18¾ sq ft) kidney-shaped pre-cast shell
18-20 x 250 mm x 250 mm (10 in x 10 in) paving slabs
50 kg (100 lb) sand
50 kg (100 lb) sand (optional)

Preparation
1. Decide where you want to sink the pond and place the shell upside down on the spot. This will enable you to incorporate the lip when you mark the outline of the shell with chalk, lime or flour (*see* page 20). A word of warning, however: if the pre-cast pond you are installing has an irregular shape, you will have to set it right-side up or you will end up with a mirror-image and the shell will not fit.

Excavation
2. Put the shell aside and dig out the soil to the full depth of the pond plus the thickness of the proposed surround; in this case 310 mm (1 ft). It will be easier to place the shell in position if you make the hole just a little wider than you have marked. If there is a shallow end, excavate that section first and then dig out the soil, gradually working towards the deeper end.

3. When excavation is complete, make sure that the base of the hole is absolutely level and that there are no stones or undulations which will prevent the shell from sitting firmly on the ground. If the earth is very stony, you can lay a shallow bed of sand (about 20 mm (¾ in) is more than adequate) over the top to cushion the weight of the pond. If this is necessary, you will have to excavate slightly deeper to accommodate the sand.

Placing the pond
4. Place the shell in the hole and use a spirit level to check that it is straight and properly aligned. You may need to remove the shell and add or scrape a little soil away to make it even.

5. The surround will sit on the lip of the pond, which should now be a little below the original ground level. Place the slabs around the pond and mark their approximate position. Remove grass and soil to a depth of about 65 mm (2½ in) to accommodate the slabs.

6. Use some of the excavated soil to backfill the gap between the sides of the shell

STEP 1

STEP 5

STEP 2

STEP 6

STEP 7

STEP 9

STEP 10

and the hole. Compact this area and the newly dug section around the perimeter of the pond. If the pond has moulded shelves for plants, take care to backfill under these areas properly. Do not worry if the interior of the pond is soiled, this is one occasion when you do not want it to look pristine.

Paving the surround

7. Deposit a layer of clean building or river sand around the excavated and compacted edge of the pond. This should be approximately 25 mm (1 in) thick once it has been compacted.

8. Smooth the sand with a straight-edged piece of wood. For drainage reasons, it is prudent to allow the top of the paved surface to slope very slightly away from the edge of the pond.

9. Lay the paving slabs on the sand without mortar. Press them firmly into place and make use of a spirit level to check that the surface of the edging as a whole is flat.

10. Fill all gaps between the slabs with soil and plant with a ground cover which will thrive in moist conditions. Pebbles pushed between the slabs can also look attractive.

Finishing off

11. Make sure the interior of the pond is clean before filling it with water and stocking with a selection of water lilies, aquatic plants and fish.

Suitable for even the smallest patio, the pond transforms what was previously a neglected corner of the garden.

A POND FOR DUCKS

Ducks will make themselves at home in just about any reasonable container of water, from a large bowl to a swimming pool. If you are building a pond specially for ducks, any construction method is suitable. Flexible pond liners probably offer the most inexpensive option. They are also reasonably quick to install and may be used for a pond of virtually any shape and size. A variety of materials are suitable for liners (*see* page 13) and before you start, investigate what is available in your area. For this project, 500 micron polyethylene sheeting was used to make a randomly-shaped duck pond. The deepest part of the pond is about 400 mm (16 in) and a 200 mm- (8 in-) deep shelf for marginal plants has been left around parts of the perimeter. A reconstituted stone surround overlaps the edges slightly, hiding the liner and giving the pond a more natural look.

STEP 5

5. Decide roughly where the plant shelf will extend and dig out the remainder of the pool to 400 mm (16 in), or, if you are going to incorporate a cushioning layer of sand, 420 mm (16½ in). If you wish, you can leave a reasonably even shelf, approximately 230 mm (9 in) wide, around the full circumference of the pond. This is not essential, however, and you may even want to create a shallow area at one end to enable you to introduce a greater number of marginal plants.

Materials
For a pond no longer than 2.8 m x 4.5 m (9 ft 2 in x 14 ft 9 in) at its longest points:
1 x 6 m x 4 m (19 ft 8 in x 13 ft) sheet polyethylene, PVC or EPDM sheeting
10 m² (12 sq yd) paving slabs
125 kg (275 lb) cement
0.5 m³ (0.6 cu yd) sand
270 kg (600 lb) sand (optional)

Preparation
1. Decide what shape you want the duck pond to be and mark out the area roughly using a garden hose or length of rope. Alternatively, use pegs to define the area, or even lime and flour. This is one occasion when absolute accuracy is not essential.

2. Once you are happy with the shape, measure the longest and widest points of the pond. You must add at least twice the proposed depth to these measurements to ensure there will be sufficient liner for construction. Rather buy a little extra than find you do not have enough once the hole has been dug.

STEP 1

Excavation
3. The first step is to remove all grass and other vegetation. If you are digging up an established lawn, you may be able to use the turfs elsewhere in the garden.

4. Now dig out 200 mm (about 8 in) of soil which will take you to the depth required for plant shelves. If you need to line the pond with a layer of sand before installing the liner (*see* step 3), you will have to remove the soil to a depth of about 220 mm (8½ in). Good quality top-soil can often be used elsewhere in the garden or, if mixed with compost, to fill containers for potted plants.

STEP 6

6. While the bottom of an informal pool of this nature does not have to be completely level, it is imperative that the surrounding edges are. If the ground on one side is higher than the other side, this will become quite obvious once the pond has been filled with water. Use pegs and a spirit level set on a straight-edged piece of wood to establish your levels from an acceptable datum point (*see* illustration on page 11).

7. Now remove soil wherever necessary, using the pegs stuck into the side of the pond wall as a guideline.

8. Double-check the depth of the pond, measuring from the lower plane of the straightedge to the earth below. If necessary, dig out more soil.

9. Inspect the sides and floor of the excavated hole and remove any sharp stones, sticks or other debris which could damage the liner.

Fitting the liner
10. If you are going to line the inside of the excavation with sand, do so now, taking care not to damage the shelves you have created.

11. Roll out the sheeting to cover the hole. It is helpful to use paving slabs or bricks to keep the liner in position, especially if you are working alone.

Ducks are at home in this simple DIY pond constructed with a polyethylene liner. The marginal shelf helps them get in and out of the water with ease.

STEP 11

12. Make sure the liner is fairly well centred and gradually drape it loosely into the hole. Anchor the edges with pavers.

13. Now fill the pond with water. As you do this, move the stones to gradually ease the sheeting so that it fits the contours of the excavation as snugly as possible. Some creasing and even minor folding is inevitable with most materials, but this is not generally a problem.

14. Once the pool is full, trim the edges of the liner, retaining enough to secure it permanently under the slabs. Leave the loose pavers or bricks in position for the time being.

Paving the surround
15. Having levelled the ground around the pond, you can lay the paving slabs without any further preparation. You must be sure that the flattened area is wide enough to accommodate the slabs. If it is not, cut back more of the grass and soil and, with the help of a spirit level, check that it is flat.

16. Mix weak mortar in the ratio 1:6, cement to sand, as described on page 26. Do not add too much water or it will weaken the mixture and make it too runny.

17. Although any paving may be used, a combination of 250 mm x 250 mm (10 in x 10 in), 250 mm x 500 mm (10 in x 20 in) and 500 mm x 500 mm (20 in x 20 in) reconstituted stone slabs creates a particularly nice effect. Lay the slabs on a 20 mm (¾ in) bed of mortar placed over any projecting plastic, once again using a spirit level to ensure they are straight. The pavers should, if possible, project over the water by about 30 mm (1 in), hiding any

exposed sheeting and limiting exposure to sunlight to a minimum. Tap the slabs gently into place using a rubber mallet.

18. If possible, clean away any mortar which may have dropped into the pond.

19. Once the mortar beneath the slabs has set thoroughly, mix a new batch of mortar and use a trowel to fill all the gaps between the slabs. If the mortar mixture falls onto the slabs, remove it with a damp cloth or sponge while it is still wet. Now trim any liner still visible beyond the paving.

Planting the pond
20. If there is a lot of mortar in the pond, you may have to drain it (*see* page 24) before refilling with fresh water. Leave the water to stand for a few days. Choose a selection of plants from the different groups mentioned on pages 32-34. If you are going to introduce ducks to this pond, avoid expensive plants which they can destroy easily.

STEP 13

STEP 15

STEP 17

CLAY-PUDDLED POND

Not only does bentonite enable you to create a beautifully natural-looking pond, it is inexpensive and relatively simple to use. No special skills are necessary, and it will take you only a few days to complete. If yours is a large pond, you would be advised to hire a compacting machine, otherwise tools are minimal. The secrets of success with a bentonite pond are to follow the guidelines carefully and to avoid working in wet weather. You will need at least three days of constant sunshine to complete this project.

STEP 3

Materials
For an irregular, metre-deep (3 ft 3 in) pond 5 m x 4 m (16 ft 5 in x 13 ft 1 in):
200 kg (440 lb) bentonite or sodium clay

Preparation
1. Mark out the perimeter of your pond to get an idea of the outline you want. The shape does not have to be as precise as in some other methods and can be changed as you start excavation if you wish.

2 . First dig out the soil to the required depth, bearing in mind that quite a lot

(200 mm/8 in) will be returned to the hole. Make sure that the walls of the pond do not slope more than 1:3. Dislodge and remove all vegetation, stones and tree stumps. You can take most of the soil away, although you will need to retain some to mix with the bentonite and to spread over the mixture once it has been compacted. There is no need to weigh the soil out, but you will need a total of 5 m³ (6 ½ cu yd), which is a hefty pile.

Construction
3. Compact the floor area of the pond with a punner or by machine. Make sure the banks are also compacted thoroughly.

STEP 4

4. Spread the bentonite powder evenly over the surface of the excavation. Each 40 kg (88 lb) bag should cover about 5 m² (6 sq yd).

5. Now spread a layer of soil about 100 mm (4 in) thick over the blanket of bentonite. You can usually utilise the excavated soil for this purpose.

STEP 2

STEP 5

Timbers rescued from an old wharf have been used to construct a rustic deck which juts out over the bentonite pond. The sediment clouding the newly filled pond will settle in time and the planted perimeter will eventually cover the bare earth to create a natural haven for wildlife.

6. Working systematically from one side of the pond to the other, thoroughly mix the bentonite and soil with a spade; or use a rake to combine the materials.

7. Compact the walls and basin of the pond for the second time. Once again, you can use a homemade punner or a compacting machine.

8. Spread a 100 mm (4 in) layer of soil over the compacted materials. This will act as a protective layer.

9. Use a hose to sprinkle water over the prepared surface, and then compact well once again.

10. Leave the pond for about 48 hours to allow the water to react with the bentonite. As the clay draws out the moisture, you will be able to see the top layer of soil drying out. This is essential if the sealing process is to be successful.

11. Wet the surface again thoroughly, with a gentle spray, after this two-day period and leave overnight.

12. The following day you can fill the pond. Do this slowly, with a fine spray, to avoid damaging the sealed surface.

STEP 6

.STEP 9

INFORMAL KOI POND

Roughly formed with concrete, this pond was specially designed to accommodate and display a small quantity of koi. It is 500 mm (1 ft 8 in) deep, the minimum required for these ornamental fish, and a biological filter has been fitted. This feature incorporates attractive man-made rocks around the perimeter. If similar fake rocks are not available in your area, a more conventional rockery could be assembled and constructed in the same way.

Materials

For this 6 m² (65 sq ft) pond:

1 x 3 m x 3 m x 6 mm (9 ft 10 in x 9 ft
    10 in x ¼ in) reinforcing mesh
250 kg (550 lb) cement
0.45 m³ (16 cu ft) sand
300 kg (8 cu ft) stone
waterproofing additive (optional)
15 litres (3 gal) rubberised bitumen
    sealer (depending on brand)

To build the rockery (optional)

2.5 m x 76 mm (8 ft 2 in x 3 in)
    galvanized metal pole
wire mesh
glassfibre reinforced cement (GRC)
    rock panels (see page 94)
    OR rocks
mortar
immersible pump, with a water head
    compatible with the rockery height
biological filter
pipework and connectors (dependent
    on configuration of rockery)
outdoor cable and conduit

Preparation

1. Decide exactly where you want the pond and mark it out with a hose or rope.

2. Knock pegs into the ground around the perimeter of the proposed pond at intervals of approximately 500 mm (1 ft 8 in). These will enable you to establish the level of the ground surrounding the pool.

3. Before you start digging the hole, establish a datum point which will enable you to mark the height of the proposed finished surface around the pond. Do this by hammering in one of the pegs inserted into the highest level of ground, so that its apex is at the correct height. Then use a

BEFORE

spirit level to accurately adjust all the other pegs so that their tops are even. If you have a dumpy level (see page 11), you can speed up and simplify this operation. You will, however, need to work with a helper.

Excavation

4. The excavation of this pond is exactly the same as all the others. However, it is more important to slope the sides slightly because of this particular method of construction. Make sure the pegs remain in position even once the hole has been dug.

Reinforcing

5. Once the hole is ready, line it with the reinforcing mesh; this steel reinforcing will make the pond more stable and help to stop it from cracking. Since this is an informal pool with an irregular shape, it will be necessary to cut some of the mesh to get it to fit. You can do this without too much effort if you use a hack-saw or bolt cutters. Bend and then push the ends you have cut into the soil to keep it in position. To ensure an even thickness of concrete, it is useful to insert small chips of brick to form spacers between the mesh and the earth.

Concrete

6. Working in batches, mix together a total of three bags of the cement and approximately 300 kg (600 lb or 8 cu ft) each of sand and stone; the correct amount of waterproofing additive (based on the manufacturer's instructions) and just enough water to make the concrete pliable. Remember to mix only as much as you can place in two hours.

7. If you are incorporating a rockery, throw a concrete slab at one end of the pond to form a supporting shelf. If you (or a landscaping specialist) are using GRC panels, it will be necessary to embed a metal pole in the centre of the slab to brace and support them. Note that a feature made with natural rocks will require more space than one made with panels.

STEP 2

STEP 8

8. Shovel the concrete mix into the hole and use a trowel followed by a float to smooth the surface.

9. The completed concrete shell should be about 80 mm (3 in) thick. Make sure that the upper lip is level with the top of the pegs previously inserted around the circumference of the pond.

10. Use a spirit level and a water level (see pages 10-11) to check that the upper surface of the shell is level. You can also use a dumpy level, but these are cumbersome and considerably more expensive.

11. Allow the concrete to set for at least 48 hours.

Plaster or render
12. You will need a good, strong render mix to finish the pond. The remaining cement and sand will give you a 1:3 mix, which is recommended not only for ponds, but for reservoirs and swimming pools as well. It is a good idea to add a waterproofing agent to this too. Use a round trowel like those employed by pool builders to render the pond. Then take a damp sponge and smooth the surface.

STEP 9

STEP 12

Pump and filter
13. Install all pipework and fit any necessary electrical connections before you finish the pond or build a rockery. While guidelines are given on pages 30 and 31, the factors involved are variable and those DIY builders without adequate experience in this field, should seek assistance from an electrician and possibly also a plumber. The pump used here is an immersible one, while the filter is hidden above ground, behind the rock feature. The 32 mm (1¼ in)

The enchanting water feature, complete with waterfall, is now the focal point. In addition, now that all the paving bricks have been removed, lush plants and an attractive fake sleeper pathway which leads to the front door of the house, add to the picture.

tubing from the pump is routed up behind the rockery with the aid of various connectors. Once installation is complete, the pump will then discharge water into a pre-cast bowl which spills into the pond.

Rockery
14. The rockery may now be constructed on the concrete shelf behind the pond. The lightweight panels are wired and welded to the metal pole in a simple, yet ingenious manner. Wire mesh is then attached between the panels, to cover all gaps.

15. Using the same 1:3 render mix, the mesh (or chicken wire) is completely covered with a roughly rendered coat. This mixture is trowelled on and then manipulated so that it blends with the moulded GRC panels.

16. When the render is completely dry, the rock feature is spray painted in colours of natural stone.

Sealing
17. Even though the waterproofing agent added to the concrete and render will ensure a reasonably waterproof shell, it is advisable to give the interior surface of the pond at least two coats of a rubberised bitumen sealant. The emulsion product used here was diluted for the first coat and applied full strength for the second.

Finishing off
18. When the bitumen is dry, fill the pond. The area around it can also be landscaped and planted. Allow all water plants to become reasonably established before introducing the koi.

STEP 14

STEP 15

NATURAL WATER GARDENS

Where water occurs naturally in the garden, very little maintainance is necessary except tidying up and weeding the area. If indigenous moisture-loving plants are already present, the water will attract all types of wildlife without any effort on your part. In properties where water is not normally present, bog gardens and wild water gardens may be ingeniously created with surprisingly little effort.

Plants in this well-established bog garden include papyrus (Cyperus papyrus), white arum lilies (Zantedeschia) and the impressive, hardy, rhubarb-like Gunnera.

When creating an informal water feature, you will presumably have tried to make it look natural. If you have followed the guidelines discussed earlier, there should be a good balance of nature in the pond, together with an interesting selection of visitors in the form of frogs, newts, dragonflies and so on. You will probably also notice an increase in the number of birds which visit your garden and, in some areas, even small animals.

Of course, if your pond was designed to accomodate expensive koi, these visitors could be a curse and you may instead be forced to cover the water with a net of some sort to discourage birds. If all these creatures are welcome guests, you can encourage their visits by creating a suitable environment for breeding.

The most desolate marshy area surrounding a stretch of open water can be transformed into a lush, treasureland of wildlife and nature by skilful planting. A boggy patch planted with appropriate flowers (marsh marigolds, for instance) will create a haven for dragonflies, bees and butterflies. Within a surprisingly short space of time you will have a wildlife pond rather than one that is ornamental.

BOG GARDENS

Even if you do not want a pond or pool, it is still possible to establish a water feature which will attract wildlife. The most obvious is a bog garden where moisture-loving plants will thrive. These 'gardens' can create a charming effect even though access may be limited.

Traditional 19th Century 'bog gardens' were often planted with rare species and located alongside contrived rock gardens. The modern version, however, frequently combines marginal aquatics with true bog and marsh plants. A natural bog garden, on the other hand, supports mainly acid-loving plants living off the layer of peat formed organically due to decomposing sphagnum and other mosses.

Natural bog and marsh gardens often adjoin ponds and pools, and this is the obvious place to create one. The inclusion of moisture-loving plants beside the pond, together with marginals just inside the pond, will help soften the edges of the water feature and thus achieve a pleasant transition between water and land. This does not mean that you cannot create a bog garden alongside a formal pond. In fact, it is one way to prevent a formal design from looking too severe.

If the soil around your pond is constantly damp, but not waterlogged, this is the perfect place for a bog garden. Even if moisture is not always present, it is a reasonably simple matter to install an underground irrigation system that will enable you to water the soil with a hose whenever it begins to dry out (see page 29). Since you are aiming to simulate marshland, this will have a more natural effect than watering from above.

One of the easiest methods of creating a bog garden is to use a plastic liner (see pages 58-59) and any of the materials mentioned on pages 13-14 may be used. You will need to perforate the base to allow for some drainage. Bury the outer edges of the plastic in the surrounding soil, without raising them right to the surface.

A bog garden can also be constructed as an extension to an existing pond. You will need to build a retaining wall between the two areas, and ensure that the soil level is at least 25 mm (1 in) above the surface of the water. A division of either loose-laid bricks or cut stone will allow water to seep slowly through to the bog garden, and a peaty soil mixture placed over a generous layer of gravel for drainage will give you a good moisture-retaining medium. You could also add compost and chipped bark to improve the quality of the soil. The main disadvantage of establishing a bog garden within the confines of a pond is the distinct possibility that the soil will be disturbed and muddy the water.

WILD WATER GARDENS

Wild gardens, including those which feature water, have become increasingly popular in recent years. Unlike the famous 'wild' gardens popularised by British gardener and author, William Robinson, more than a century ago, they are no longer intensely cultivated, with numerous exotic species. Instead, the wild garden of today is a place where various creatures and indigenous plants are encouraged to live and grow in harmony. It is also very informal and even slightly disordered.

Water features designed to attract wildlife should be as natural in appearance as possible. Ponds sealed by clay puddling and edged with grass are ideal, and a gently sloping pebble beach will give safe access to amphibians, birds and small mammals that come to the water's edge to drink. If you prefer a solid surface underfoot, use slate or simulated stone slabs, perhaps with plants between them. Timber is also suitable, and a deck or jetty can provide the perfect viewing point.

The pond should incorporate a variety of levels, as well as fairly generous marginal shelves for planting. Alternatively, the walls of the structure should slope very gradually so that soil can be spread over them to encourage plant growth. If you choose to use a flexible liner, particular care should be taken not to puncture or damage the material in any way when splitting and separating mature plants.

Even a small pre-cast pond can be planted to encourage wildlife although it is not ideal; a marshy area next to the pond will make it more effective.

WILDLIFE

Both natural and man-made wetlands will be a magnet for birds, frogs and other wildlife, while fish will help reduce numbers of unwanted insects. Even a small pond in a suburban garden will encourage all kinds of creatures to visit.

It does not take long for ponds to become naturally populated with insects, amphibians and small animals. Various beetles, worms and snails as well as water mites, dragonflies and the smaller damselflies, frogs, toads and newts will soon make their way to the water. You can introduce them from natural pools and streams, as long as you take care not to overstock your pond. Make sure you avoid pests, which include certain beetles and snails. It pays to know a little about these creatures; for instance, the larvae or nymphs of the beautiful dragonfly are so ugly and unlikely in appearance that some pond owners destroy them in ignorance. Since they can spend as long as three to four years underwater before emerging as adults, this can be a tragedy.

Reeds along the bank of a pond will encourage water shrews, voles and fieldmice to nest, and these in turn may lure the harmless grass snake to the area.

Long grass and dense plant cover will also be a haven for amphibians which spend part of their life cycle out of the water. Rocks and boulders placed to create nooks and crannies will be good resting places for these creatures.

Of course, the frogs, newts and toads you attract to your water garden will vary depending on where you live. In general, frogs are smoother and more moist than warty toads, which can spend more time away from water. Newts, with their long tails, are not as common as frogs or toads.

Fish will introduce colour and movement to the pond and are useful as they eat the eggs and larvae of mosquitoes, gnats and midges. Although various freshwater fishes are found in natural ponds and rivers, the most suitable ornamental species for a wildlife pond is probably the goldfish. These are usually inexpensive, hardy and do not need a great deal of attention.

Many of the larger birds, including herons and seagulls, should be discouraged from wildlife ponds, but most garden birds will do no harm. If you have a waterfall, you can provide a rock shelf where birds can drink and preen.

Ducks and other waterfowl can prove a menace in a pool of this nature. They eat all kinds of insects as well as small fish and plants, and they churn up mud. If you want to keep ducks, build a pond specifically for them in their own territory and do not expect too much else from it.

A man-made wetland, incorporating a pond sealed with bentonite, is guaranteed to attract birds and other wildlife.

BOG GARDEN

Although built as a separate unit, this bog garden is close enough to the adjacent pond to appear as if it is a natural extension. Construction is elementary and will not take long. Any flexible liner is suitable and the bog garden will be most successful if you install underground irrigation to keep the soil moist in the most natural way. The most challenging part may be planting it with suitable species. Although a bog garden can extend right around the perimeter of a pond, it should not be too wide.

Materials

For a bog garden measuring about 2.5 m by 1.5 m (8 ft 2 in and 4 ft 11 in):

3 m x 2 m (10 ft x 6 ft 7 in) 500 micron black polyethylene sheeting
125 kg (275 lb) gravel or crushed stone
2.5 m x 12 mm (8 ft 2 in x ½ in) semi-rigid tubing
1 x stopper
1 x hose connection
peat and river stones (optional)

Preparation

1. Decide where your bog garden is to be situated and excavate to a depth of at least 300 mm (1 ft). Keep the soil on one side, as you will later need to return at least half of it to the hole.

STEP 1

An undeveloped bed adjacent to a pond is the perfect site for a bog garden.

Excavation

2. Cover the excavation with plastic and bury the edges in the soil. It does not matter if the liner does not extend right to the top of the hole, but it must be securely anchored to prevent it from collapsing.

3. Make a few drainage holes in the bottom of the plastic with a small screwdriver or nail. The water will drain out surprisingly quickly if there are too many holes or if they are too big.

STEP 2

STEP 3

STEP 4

STEP 5

Drainage
4. Spread a layer of gravel or crushed stone over the base. This should be about 50 mm (2 in) thick.

5. Perforate the length of semi-rigid tubing to supply irrigation and plug one end. Attach the hose connection to the other end and place the tubing in the hole, allowing it to protrude at a convenient yet inconspicuous point.

STEP 6

Planting
6. You can now return some of the soil to the hole, preferably mixed half and half with peat (*see* page 32) or a good quality mushroom compost.

7. Finally plant the bog garden with suitable species. Remember to connect the hose to the buried tubing to give the plants a regular soaking, but do not allow the area to become waterlogged.

Small, round river stones have been used to define the perimeter of this attractive little bog garden.

MOVING WATER

For many, the sound of splashing water from either a fountain feature or a cascade or waterfall, thrills the senses. While still, reflective pools have a soothing effect. The element of moving water adds excitement, and even the tiniest trickle of water in a stream will make a delightful impression.
No matter where you live, it is possible to create moving water features in a range of styles, both large and small, for patios and gardens.

Fountains (*see* pages 66-79) are ornamental and often formal in style, but most other moving water appears natural in the correct environment. The most successful man-made streams, as well as the waterfalls and rockeries which go with them, are designed to imitate nature, and it pays to take time to study water features which have occurred naturally.

Unless you are lucky enough to have a natural spring or river on your property, you will need a pump to move the water to a height where gravity can take over. It then flows back into the pond and is recirculated over and over again. In addition, this equipment will aerate the pond, which is a bonus for fish. The small submersible pumps which are frequently sold with fountain fittings are adequate for the smaller water feature, but a more ambitious arrangement will require a more powerful submersible pump or even one which is located on the surface near the water (*see* page 30). You may even need more than one pump where, for instance, a waterfall flows into a pond, and from there to a stream and a second pond.

Whether you are constructing a waterfall or a cascade, it is important that as little water as possible escapes as it flows over and off the rocks and spillways. If there are leaks, or the water splashes excessively, you may find it necessary to install a top-up system in the pond to rectify these problems (*see* page 29).

It is worth remembering that some aquatic plants, water lilies in particular, do not like currents and splashing water.

Waterfalls are a popular feature of informal ponds and may be successfully linked to man-made watercourses and streams. A succession of informal cascades can be particularly effective.

The simplest way to construct a waterfall is to first build up a rockery and then pipe the water to a concealed point at the apex. The pump, which should be placed in an accessible spot at the lowest point of the waterfall, will activate the flow of water over the rocks. You can increase both audible and visual splashing by placing additional boulders in the pond at the bottom of the waterfall. Remember that the higher the rock feature, the stronger the pump must be.

Of course, the more natural your rockery appears, the more impressive the waterfall will be. You will have to cement the rocks in place, but do this carefully, so the mortar is not obvious.

In nature, the rocks over which water cascades and falls are not solid or impermeable. However, you will need to prevent

An interesting man-made waterway constructed from simulated rocks.

stepped pools lined with concrete, softening the edges with rocks and plants to achieve a more natural effect.

Pre-formed cascade units, although widely available in Britain, are not found in all countries. Made from the same materials as pre-cast ponds (*see* pages 48-49), they can be rapidly installed, but must be sensitively positioned to look natural. They are also relatively small and might be inappropriate in some environments.

Streams do not require much space, although they are generally more effective if there is room for them to meander. The course a man-made stream follows should be as natural as possible, so remember that in nature water generally takes the line of least resistance, except where it is forced around natural obstacles like rocks.

The size of any stream you decide to create must, of course, be in proportion to the garden and any other water features,

Water cascades from one level to another, creating the impression of a sheet of water.

This water feature incorporates a waterfall.

unnecessary water loss, so it is best to seal the surface over which your water flows. Furthermore, the rocks should be set on a waterproofed concrete foundation. Unless you are using very large rocks, it is often best to create the watercourse with concrete first, and then construct the rockery.

Although liners may be used to cover the course of a waterfall, they should be very well camouflaged or they will spoil the whole effect. Bitumen is fail-safe, but it, too, looks rather ugly when it is exposed. A rich render mix to which a waterproofing agent has been added, and possibly a coat of polyurethane sealant, will definitely look more attractive.

Cascades can be constructed in a more formal style. They may, for instance, imitate the Japanese 'sheet' waterfall, or the water staircase which appeared in many French and Italian gardens in previous centuries. They can also be part of a more natural water feature in the form of spillways (*see* pages 64-65) or weirs which regulate the flow of the water.

Whereas the majority of waterfalls rely on rocks and channels as a watercourse, a formal cascade feature will often include a series of flat lips. These may be made from various materials including slate, sheets of fibrecement, and even metal. You may even prefer to construct a succession of

and it need not be particularly deep. You can include a number of ponds and weirs along the course of the stream to add interest. You will need a steady supply of water to feed it and the pump (or pumps) used must have sufficient capacity to adequately recirculate the volume of water required for a constant flow.

A more contrived watercourse may be channelled rather like a mini-canal, incorporating fountains and formal cascades. Although any type of watercourse can be constructed with concrete, a stream may be very successfully created using clay or bentonite (*see* pages 52-53), provided it is reasonably slow flowing.

WANDERING WATERCOURSE

This meandering watercourse flows between man-made ponds in an expansive garden. Although there is no obvious movement, it is in fact pumped, and aeration of the water keeps it so clear you can see the river stones at the base of the stream. Construction is relatively simple, although it is a labour-intensive project. Pump requirements will depend on the size of the feature.

Materials

For a watercourse measuring approximately 5 m x 1 m (16 ft 5 in x 3 ft 2 in) and 800–900 mm (about 3 ft) deep:

600 kg (1 320 lb) cement
0.9 m³ (1 cu yd) sand
0.9 m³ (1 cu yd) crushed stone
waterproofing additive
15 litres (3¼ gal) rubberised bitumen sealer (optional)
river stones

Preparation

1. Lay out the watercourse in keeping with the landscaping plan of your garden as a whole. Mark it in some way, preferably with builder's line or string and pegs. Alternatively, lay out the course with river stones.

2. Dig out the soil to a depth of 1 m (3 ft) ensuring that the sides of the excavation slope gradually outwards (or you will find it difficult to line with concrete without additional reinforcing or shuttering). Remove the soil.

Concrete

3. Compact the excavation well with a punner.

4. Now mix the concrete in batches in the ratio 1:2:2 of cement, sand and stone, and then add the waterproofing medium and water. Note that the quantity of waterproofing medium will depend on what you are using; follow the manufacturer's instructions.

5. Line the excavation with a 100 mm- (4 in-) thick layer of concrete; flatten and compact it as described on page 54.

6. After at least 48 hours, when the concrete has thoroughly set, you can paint it with bitumen. This will be an additional precaution against water leaking.

Stones

7. When the bitumen is dry, line the walls and basin of the concrete course with river stones. Lay them like a dry stone wall, with the larger ones at the bottom and smaller ones on top.

Finishing off

8. For a natural look, you will need to plant marsh-loving species along the banks of the watercourse. Grasses may be encouraged to grow up to its edges. You could also build a simple bridge to enable you to cross the stream at some point.

One side of the bank has been planted with moisture-loving plants while grass has been allowed to grow over the stones on the opposite side.

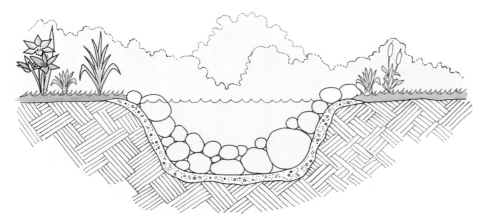

Cross-section of the completed watercourse.

SPLASHING WATERFALL

A charming, natural-looking waterfall links two ponds constructed at different levels of a sloping garden. Both ponds were built with concrete and then plastered, and a series of rocks cemented into place around the edges to hide the structure. Plants further soften the effect. The rocks which form the course of the waterfall, have been secured on concrete steps between the ponds. As the concrete has been made impervious, there is no need to waterproof the rocks. Materials quantified are for the waterfall only, and not the ponds.

4. Concrete around one end of the rock and lay another 100 mm (4 in) of the mixture along the second step. Set the second rock in position, sloping it in the same way as before. Repeat this procedure, using the smallest rock at the top.

5. Finally concrete smaller rocks into place along the edges of the rockery and around the perimeter of the ponds.

Pump
6. The pump may be concealed in the collecting pond and cables run to a waterproof box or the nearest plug point. Make sure it is accessible so that you do not have to wade into the water to remove it for cleaning or repairs.

7. Connect the tubing to the pump and run it underground to the top pond, and lead it into the water about 500 mm (1 ft 8 in) from the apex of the waterfall.

Materials
120 kg (265 lb) cement
245 kg (0.25 cu yd) sand
245 kg (540 lb) stone
waterproofing additive
large rocks and boulders
10 m x 20 mm (11 yd x ¾ in)
   semi-rigid tubing
1 x submersible pump
outdoor cable and conduit

Preparation
1. Mark out the position of the rockery and cut three steps into the slope. The dimensions of each step will depend on the size of the boulders you have, as well as the slope. Although instructions are not given here, you should mark out and prepare for construction of the ponds at the same time.

Concrete
2. Concrete the surface of the collecting pond first as described on pages 22-24, then start working from the bottom of the rockery. You will need to mix the cement, sand and stone in the ratio 1:2:2 with waterproofing additive and water. Be sure to use sufficient additive or the waterfall will leak.

3. You will need at least three large, flat-topped rocks for the rockery, and so it is inevitable you will require assistance. Lay about 100 mm (4 in) of concrete on the lowest step, compact with a straightedge and, while the mixture is still wet, place the first rock in position (see illustration), so that it slopes forward very slightly.

Not only does a waterfall look attractive in the garden, it also increases the oxygen level in the pond which is advantageous for both fishes and plants.

Cross-section of the waterfall constructed on three tiers.

MULTIPLE CASCADE

Instead of the usual pond with rockeries and a waterfall supplied with recirculating water, this multiple cascade is made up of eight tiered pools of varying sizes, five of which incorporate slate spillways. It was constructed with huge boulders and rocks found on the site, and is operated from a power point in a concealed waterproof box behind one of the rocks. The pools, all of which are made from handpacked concrete, are irregular in size, with the largest in front and smallest on the upper tier. The five upper ponds are all fed from the pump which is positioned in a corner of the biggest pool. The basic design may be used on any sloping site, although it will have to be adapted, depending on the natural materials available. The actual size of the spillways is not important, although they should be in proportion to the feature as a whole, and must overlap the water below.

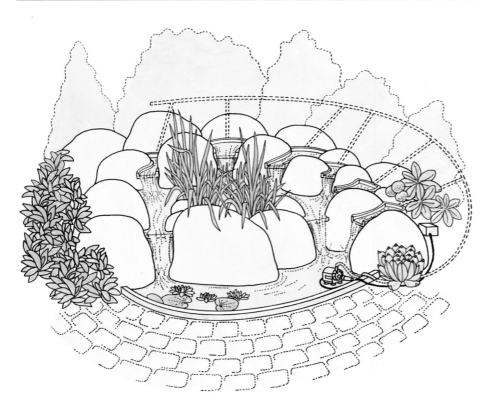

An elevated layout of the multiple cascade.

Materials

This feature covers approximately 64 m² (76 sq yd), and is 2.5-3 m (8-10 ft) high with an island in the centre.
Boulders and rocks
3 750 kg (8 267 lb) cement
5.2 m³ (6.8 cu yd) sand
5 m³ (6.5 cu yd) stone
waterproofing additive (depending on brand used)
40 litres (8¾ gal) rubberised bitumen sealer (optional)
reinforcing mesh

1 x 700 mm x 500 mm x 30 mm (2 ft 4 in x 1 ft 8 in x 1¼ in) cut slate or similar material (a)
1 x 600 mm x 520 mm x 30 mm (2 ft x 1 ft 8 in x 1¼ in) cut slate or similar material (b)
1 x 600 mm x 500 mm x 30 mm (2 ft x 1 ft 8 in x 1¼ in) cut slate or similar material (c)
1 x 600 mm x 320 mm x 30 mm (2 ft x 1 ft x 1¼ in) cut slate or similar material (d)
1 x 600 mm x 300 mm x 30 mm (2 ft x 1 ft 1¼ in) cut slate or similar material (e)
1 x 540 mm x 400 mm x 30 mm (1 ft 9 in x 1 ft 4 in x 1¼ in) cut slate or similar material (f)
1 x 400 mm x 300 mm x 30 mm (1 ft 4 in x 1 ft x 1¼ in) cut slate or similar material (g)
1 x submersible pump
30 m x 20 mm (33 yd x ¾ in) flexible pipe
4 x T-pieces
silicone sealer
waterproof electrical box
outdoor cable and conduit

Preparation

1. The site must be terraced and all the large rocks and boulders set in position. This cascade is constructed on three levels, and some of the earth will have to be shifted. If the boulders occur naturally, you may be able to create a water feature around them; you may even need some mechanical help to position large rocks.

2. Once you have the basic layout in place, dig out the eight pools to the required depth. The largest, which is located at the base of the feature, is also the deepest (about 500 mm or 1 ft 8 in). The small upper pools range from 300-200 mm (1 ft-8 in), while the two central pools are approximately 300 mm (1 ft) deep.

The multiple cascade, constructed with natural rocks and boulders on slightly sloping ground.

Pipework

3. The next step is to position the pipework which will feed the cascades. The pump will lie in the bottom pond while the pipe runs up from there, leading off from a T-piece to each of the upper pools (*see* illustration on page 64).

4. You will need to lead pipework into the five top pools from below. Allow the pipework to protrude by about 150 mm (6 in) in each case. Once the pools have been concreted and rendered, these points should not leak. If they do, use silicone to seal around them later.

Concrete

5. Line each of the eight excavations with reinforcing mesh as described on page 23, and then mix the concrete in the usual 1:2:2 ratio with waterproofing additive. For a water feature this size, you will need more than 68 pockets of cement, so it may be worth considering having it delivered ready-mixed. Otherwise think about hiring a concrete mixer.

6. Line the pools in exactly the same way as described for the project on pages 54-55, covering the edges of the rocks as well as the excavated soil. The walls should all be about 100 mm (4 in) thick and it is vital that they are completely watertight, or the

feature will leak. Also remember to ensure that all outer edges of individual pools are level. Although you will need to use a spirit level throughout the construction process, you will find a water level is also invaluable, especially as you are working on three different levels.

Plaster or render

7. It will take about 48 hours for the concrete to set, after which you can render it.

One of the slate cascades.

Add waterproofing additive to the 1:3 cement to sand mix to ensure the shells will be impermeable. Apply the render with a round trowel to make the job easier.

8. Also cement the slate spillways in place, rounding off the edges to neaten them. Make certain they overlap the structure below to ensure that the water will spill into the pool and not onto the rocks.

Sealing

9. Once the render has set, you can paint the interior surfaces with bitumen or polyurethane if you wish.

Finishing off

10. Attach the open end of the piping to the pump and position it in a corner of the lowest pond. Since a large, fairly powerful submersible pump will be needed for a feature of this size, you may need to camouflage it with loose rocks.

11. The waterproof power box may be concealed in the top section of the rockery and underground conduiting run to the house. The pump cable can then be led inconspicuously over or around the rocks and plugged in.

12. Finally, add the plants of your choice, fill the pools, and switch on the pump.

FOUNTAINS

There is a wide range of fountains available, and your choice will enable you to introduce instant sound and movement to the garden or patio. The ornamental design of many pre-cast products will add charm and character to the area, while the fountain jet itself may be exploited as a form of living sculpture. Whether you choose to install a fountain as a feature on its own or as part of a larger water garden, the procedures to be followed are the same.

For many centuries, fountains were an essential element of garden design. They were found in the inner courtyards of ancient communities, often constructed as the focal point in Medieval gardens and they marked the centrepoint in many European towns and villages. A number of the great 16th and 17th Century castles, villas and mansions in Britain and Europe boasted spectacular designs (*see* page 7).

Contemporary fountains are constructed on a much smaller scale, and are frequently found in gardens created in a particular style. Italianate gardens, for instance, invariably display lavish designs with flourishes of water; fountains incorporating statuary are the order of the day in those established in the Victorian genre; and simple bamboo fountains are frequently found in the Japanese-style garden.

Whatever its design, a fountain will introduce sound and movement to the garden or patio, and capture the exhilarating combination of light and water.

While most fountains are appropriate to the formal pool, many pre-cast units are equally suitable as a water feature on their own. Designs range from the grand and classical designs, which incorporate tiers and extravagant ornamentation, to simple bird-baths converted to accommodate a variety of fountain heads.

There is a suitable fountain for every type of outdoor area, from the smallest townhouse patio to the largest property incorporating rolling lawns and lakes.

Although many pre-cast fountains are freestanding, some of the most attractive designs may be wallmounted, creating ideal decorations for courtyards and patio areas. Alternatively, you may prefer to make your own feature using bowls, sealed plant pots, wooden tubs, or any other suitable containers.

You may prefer to dispense with ornamentation completely and install your fountain fittings so that the water jets out of the pond itself, or perhaps spurts over an expanse of pebbles.

Whatever your choice, you will need a suitable pump, powerful enough to shoot the spray above the container to the desired height. Submersible pumps are quite adequate for most garden fountains, and if you want to activate more than one at a time, it may be sensible to opt for a robust surface pump. You may have to utilise one of these larger pieces of equipment if a very high head of water is required, as in a sizeable, multi-tiered construction. A fountain incorporated in a swimming pool arrangement may be operated by the pool pump.

Spurting wall-mounted fountains do not require a jet nozzle, but upward-spraying water features usually incorporate these

A simple fountain, mounted on a wall, squirts into a shallow brick pond.

A pre-cast concrete fountain is set in the top pool of this attractive water feature.

simple mechanisms to add interest. The jet fitting chosen will depend on the particular effect you wish to achieve. There are many different spray patterns available including bell-, dome- and tulip-shaped jets, as well as multi-tiered spray jets which are designed to create a swirling effect, and foam jets which create the impression of a bubbling geyser.

There is, of course, nothing to prevent you from alternating one or two of these from time to time, depending on your mood or the occasion.

Connection to the pump is simple, although you may need to attach an additional length of tubing between the two units to camouflage the pump properly (*see* page 31).

Although the appeal of most water features is in their natural beauty, illuminated fountains can add something quite special to patios and other outdoor areas. An underwater lamp, for instance, may be hidden in such a way that it creates a dramatic effect at night.

Self-contained illuminated designs may incorporate a spotlight encased in a waterproof container, with different coloured lenses so you can change the colour of the light. Some manufacturers have developed revolving lights which produce an interesting kaleidoscope of colour.

An elaborate fountain positioned as the focal point of an entrance patio.

BIRD-BATH FOUNTAIN

This project proves that even the simplest bird bath can make a pleasing and versatile water feature. While most bird baths are made from pre-cast concrete, this one was moulded from much lighter fibrecement, then painted to look like marble. You will find that most bird baths are suitable for fountain use, and that many manufacturers of pre-cast products will convert them for you by inserting a pipe or tubing through the stem. Since it is a free-standing unit, this one has been set in a large bowl. If a catchment bowl is not supplied with the bird bath, use any suitable watertight container, or secure the fountain to a plinth in a pond. Just make sure it does not fall over. Note that the pump which activates the various water jets is hidden in the base of the hollow stem of this bird bath.

Materials
pre-cast bird bath and bowl
1 x 520 mm x 12 mm (20 in x ½ in) flexible tubing
1 x submersible pump, with 700 mm (2 ft 4 in) water head
fountain heads
outdoor cable and conduit

Preparation
1. Unless your bird bath has already been converted into a fountain, the first step will be to drill a hole in the centre of the upper dish to accommodate the pipework. Remember that 12 mm (½ in) tubing has an exterior diameter of about 16 mm (⅝ in), and the hole should be wide enough to accommodate this. You must also use the correct drill bit for the material you are drilling.

2. Push the tubing through the bottom of the supporting stem and the hole you have drilled in the dish or bowl of the bird bath. Secure it in position with a suitable two-part epoxy putty and, when this is dry, seal the upper surface with silicone or something similar.

3. If you want to paint the bird bath, or give it an appropriate paint finish, do so now. Make sure that the paint is water resistant and, if you plan to stock the pond or collecting bowl with fish or plant life, that it is also non-toxic. Rinse the surface thoroughly before filling.

4. Establish the position of the nearest electrical connection and take the necessary steps to ensure you can operate the fountain safely once it has been installed. You will need a sealed power point close to the fountain, or waterproof cable which runs into the house (see page 30). If required, enlist the assistance of a qualified electrician.

STEP 1

Installation
5. Having decided where your fountain is to be located, check that the site is absolutely level, which is probably the case with an existing hard surface. If you are placing it on an established lawn or in a garden bed, any uneven earth will have to be removed. If it is to be set in an existing pond, you may have to drain the water and build a plinth with bricks and mortar, or you may be able to simply set it on bricks or blocks. If there is any danger of instability, you will have to cement the fountain in place.

STEP 5

6. Using a sharp utility knife, trim the tubing which extends out of the dish. Make sure you leave enough exposed to attach the various fountain fittings.

STEP 6

7. Remember that the power of the pump chosen should be compatible with the height of the bird bath; for instance, a pump with a water head of 700 mm (2 ft 4 in) is suitable for this 500 mm (1 ft 8 in) high design. When attaching the pump, you will probably have to trim the other end of the tubing before joining it to the

The fountain feature has been positioned under a tree to attract birds.

outlet. If the tubing is not the correct diameter for the outlet, you may have to use a reducer of some sort.

8. Now you can fill the catchment bowl with water.

Operating the fountain

9. Before you activate the fountain, decide which jet type you want and slide it onto the pipe.

10. Your pump can now be plugged into a power point and switched on. Sit back and enjoy the different patterns your fountain heads create.

STEP 9

The pipe spurts without an additional jet.

STEP 7

A dome-shaped jet creates an attractive effect.

PRE-CAST FOUNTAIN FEATURE

Perhaps the most popular fountains are those which comprise a pre-cast pond and some kind of ornamental structure with pedestal which sits in it and stands against a wall. Like the Bird-Bath Fountain on pages 68-69, these are easy to erect. and the myriad designs available make them suitable for most applications. Although many of the pre-cast versions are free-standing, several designs can be placed against a wall, which makes them a particularly good choice for the smaller garden or townhouse patio. There is, of course, nothing to stop you installing this type of fountain in a pond or in the garden itself, although you may first need to establish a solid and level surface to accommodate it.

STEP 2

STEP 5

Materials
pre-cast fountain (pond, pedestal, bowl and gargoyle)
cement-based adhesive
heavy-duty hook with Rawl plug
1 x 1.7 m x 10 mm (5 ft 6 in x ⅜ in) flexible tubing
1 x submersible pump, with 1.4 m (4 ft 6 in) water head
outdoor cable and conduit

Preparation
1. Before you do anything else, make sure you have access to a power point.

2. Decide where you want to erect the fountain and, if necessary, measure the distance from each end of the wall, to ensure it will be centred. If you are building a solid base for the fountain, it is essential to first mark the position of the pond.

3. The next step to tackle is to ensure that the surface beneath your fountain is absolutely flat and level. If your paving or hard surface slopes, you will have to build a low plinth with bricks and mortar, or with concrete cast *in situ* (*see* page 22). Slight imperfections in gradient can be rectified with a little mortar, held in place with shuttering while it dries.

4. Many pre-cast concrete fountains are made to accommodate pipework in the centre of the pedestal, if it is freestanding, or behind the bowl, as is the case with this design. If necessary, make a groove by cutting carefully with an angle grinder. It is important that the tubing does not kink and prevent the water from flowing freely.

Installation
5. Position the pedestal in the centre at the back of the pond and use a spirit level to ensure that it is vertical. Pre-cast products may be uneven, which adds charm, but can make installation rather difficult. As each section of the fountain balances on the next, the pedestal must be straight.

The pre-cast concrete fountain, which is supplied in four sections, is to be erected alongside a wall.

STEP 7

STEP 10

STEP 11

6. If the pedestal is not perfectly straight and upright, you can lodge chips of stone under the base when you cement it into its permanent position. To do this, you can use a strong, dry-cement screed or a cement-based adhesive. Only a small quantity is required, and it should be a relatively dry mixture.

7. Smooth the edges of the adhesive with a trowel and check that the top of the pedestal is level. Allow to dry overnight.

8. Once the pedestal is secure, the scalloped bowl can be cemented into position. To ensure that the water overflows into the pond and does not splash onto the surrounding paving, the bowl is set so that it tips forward very slightly. Nevertheless, the back of the container must be level, as this, in turn, will support the spurting gargoyle.

9. Since this fountain is designed to be erected against a wall, the gargoyle must be securely attached in some way. This one is made to hang and you will have to drill into the wall and bolt a heavy-duty hook in position. By using a hook, rather

than a straight bolt, you will allow the top panel to fall forward slightly which will, in turn, affect the flow of the water.

10. Before you hang the gargoyle, position the tubing behind the fountain structure so that it fits snugly into the groove behind the scalloped bowl. Allow sufficient tubing to protrude above this container so that you can push it through the gargoyle's mouth.

11. Now hang the gargoyle on the hook, pushing the length of tubing carefully

through the hole from behind. If it is too long, you can trim it with a utility knife so that it is flush with the opening.

12. Fill the pond. You can also pour a little water into the scallop to facilitate the flow.

Operating the fountain
13. Check that the pump has the correct water head for your fountain. Connect the tubing to your pump as previously described and plug the pump into the power point provided. Switch on and enjoy the soothing trickle of water.

STEP 8

Terracotta pots and a stencilled trellis with wisteria add the finishing touches.

WALL-MOUNTED FOUNTAIN

Various pre-cast, wall-mounted fountains are available. Some, like this one, are supplied in two parts, but assembled as one unit, while others, also consisting of an ornamental outlet and catchment container, are secured to the wall at two separate points. Some are moulded as a single unit, with a head of some kind and a basin. While the basic installation is the same for all designs, the pipework of a two-part fountain will have to be embedded in the wall as illustrated in the Pond with Planters on pages 42-43. Apart from the fountain itself, minimal materials are required for this project. Note, however, that the number and size of screws and other accessories may alter according to the design.

STEP 1

STEP 2

Materials
pre-cast fountain for mounting
  on a wall
4 x No. 8 x 50 mm (2 in) screws
4 x M8 Rawl plugs
1 x 1 m x 10 mm (1 yd x ⅜ in)
  flexible tubing
1 x submersible pump, with 700 mm
  (2 ft 4 in) water head (or less)
outdoor cable and conduit

Preparation
1. Decide exactly where your fountain is to be mounted and mark a vertical line on the wall using a carpenter's pencil and spirit level for accuracy.

2. Now use a retractable tape to measure the point where the top (or bottom) of the fountain will be positioned. This one will be affixed about 200 mm (8 in) from the

top of a 1.8 m- (6 ft-) high wall. Measure the full height of the mould and mark the position of its lowest point on the wall.

3. Before you attach anything to the wall, mark where the top of the basin will be positioned on the wall. Since it is essential that your container is absolutely straight, use a spirit level rather than rely on your own judgement.

4. Pre-drill two holes in the basin, using the appropriate bit for the material you are working with – in this particular case, a masonry bit. Also make absolutely sure that the bit is the correct size for the screws you are using.

An uninteresting expanse of wall at the end of a raised patio.

STEP 4

STEP 5

STEP 6

5. Attach the basin to the wall, double-checking that it is absolutely level.

6. Insert the tubing through the lion's mouth, ensuring there is sufficient to extend to the pump below.

7. Screw the top panel to the wall as before. Make certain the bottom connects snugly with the basin and that the sides are perfectly vertical. Since there is a slight gap between the panel and the wall, you can ease the tubing into position so that it protrudes between the two sections of the

STEP 7

Proof that even the simplest wall-mounted fountain can add charm and instant ambience to any patio, however plain and ordinary.

fountain. Make absolutely sure there are no kinks in the tubing or the water will not be able to flow properly.

8. Using a sharp utility knife, trim the tubing so that it does not extend beyond the lion's mouth.

9. Attach the pump outlet and tubing.

10. Now fill your fountain with water.

11. You will need to plug the pump into a nearby power point to operate the fountain. There are various way of doing this (see page 30 for more information).

STEP 9

BOWL FOUNTAIN

Unusual fountain arrangements for small patios and courtyards are not always available ready-made. However, with a little imagination you can create something quite special using pots, bowls or even wooden tubs, provided they are watertight. This project does not require any building skills and can be completed in a few hours. The three pre-cast, fibrecement bowls used here were manufactured as pot plant containers and so drainage holes had to be sealed before the fountain could be assembled. Refer to page 17 for more information on the range of waterproofing solutions.

Materials

3 suitable containers approximately 600 mm (2 ft) in diameter, 300 mm (1 ft) high.
34-36 bricks
1 x 100 mm x 12 mm (4 in x ½ in) semi-rigid tubing
1 x 1.5 m x 10 mm (5 ft x ⅜ in) flexible tubing
4 x 100 mm x 16 mm (4 in x ⅝ in) rigid PVC pipe
1 x submersible pump, with 1.4 m (4 ft 6 in) water head
fountain head
outdoor cable and conduit
river rocks and stones (optional)

Preparation

1. Establish where the power point is to be located and ensure a suitable electrical connection is available.

2. Use a two-part epoxy putty to seal any drainage holes in two of the containers. The third bowl should have a central aperture through which you can insert tubing to attach the fountain head. If necessary, drill a hole of about 16 mm (⅝ in) in the base of one of the bowls.

3. If you plan to paint the bowls, you can do so once the putty is totally dry.

4. Using the appropriate masonry bit, drill two holes 100 mm (4 in) apart, about 35 mm (1¼ in) below the rim in the bowl with the central aperture, and in one of the sealed bowls. These measurements relate to the distance between the centres of the holes. They must be absolutely level with one another to ensure that the water flows through them evenly. To accommodate PVC pipe with a 16 mm (⅝ in) bore, you will need to drill holes approximately 20 mm (¾ in) in diameter.

STEP 5

5. Use a hack-saw to trim the end of each piece of pipe so that it forms a diagonal spout. Sand the rough edges and insert the pipe into the four holes.

6. Use two-part epoxy putty to secure each piece of pipe at a very slight angle. Again, each pair must be fitted in exactly the same way or the flow of water is likely to be uneven.

7. Insert the semi-rigid tubing into the central aperture of the first bowl and secure with putty.

Installation

8. You can, of course, build plinths for the bowls with bricks and mortar, but it is quite adequate to place them on loosely stacked bricks. To create a stepped effect, the back stack should be approximately 300 mm (1 ft) high and the middle one, 150 mm (6 in). It is essential to leave a space in the centre of the highest plinth, as well as a slight gap in the front of the third course for the tubing. You must also make certain that the base you provide for the containers supports them adequately. If your containers are of different dimensions, alter the size of the plinth as required or stack accordingly.

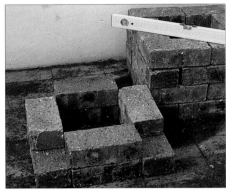

STEP 8

9. Use a spirit level to ensure that each stack of bricks is even and well balanced.

10. Before you set the bowls in position, push the flexible tubing securely into the tube epoxied into the base of the first bowl. Place this container on the highest plinth and carefully push the tubing through the gap left in the third course of loosely laid bricks.

11. Set the remaining two bowls in place. Carefully position the spouts of the upper bowls so that they spill water into each lower bowl. Check levels with a spirit level.

STEP 11

12. Put the pump in the lowest bowl, with its outlet facing upwards, and join the flexible tubing to the outlet.

13. Attach the fountain head to the tubing in the top container.

14. As the pump, tubing and power cable leading from the pump will all be visible, you will want to camouflage them in some way. The simplest solution is to place river rocks and stones in each of the three bowls and set pot plants around the water feature.

15. Fill the three containers with water.

Operating the fountain

16. For a feature placed close to the house, it is a simple matter to lead wiring from an inside plug point, through a conduit to an external plug point (*see* page 30). Now all you need to do is plug in the pump and switch on the electricity.

Exposed pipework and a dilapidated wooden tub do nothing to enhance the paved area next to the front entrance of a suburban home.

An imaginative three-tiered fountain arrangement now enlivens the entrance, adding colour and plant life. Round river stones and greenery in pots disguise the pipes, bricks, conduit and external plug box.

PEBBLE FOUNTAIN

Pebble fountains make simple yet effective garden displays. They do not take up much space, so may be sited in the smallest area; alternatively, they may be included in a much larger landscaping scheme. You can site a pebble fountain in lawn, although it will be easier to maintain if located in a garden bed. Alternatively, sink the reservoir prior to paving a patio and incorporate it as a feature.

STEP 4

Materials

container approximately 560 mm (1 ft 10 in) in diameter, 310 mm (1 ft) high
plastic pot, 200 mm (8 in) in diameter, 180 mm (7 in) high
1 x submersible pump, with 1.4 m (4 ft 6 in) water head
1 x 350 mm x 12 mm (1 ft 2 in x ½ in) semi-rigid tubing
fountain heads (optional)
outdoor cable and conduit (optional)
river stones
rounded pebbles

Preparation

1. You will need to build or install a reservoir to hold water below ground level. You can construct this with bricks and mortar and then render and seal it with bitumen or polyuretane, or simply sink a watertight container in the ground. A bowl-shaped planter made from fibrecement was used here, so the drain hole in the centre of the base had to plugged with epoxy putty.

2. Decide where the water feature is to be built and then either peg or mark out the area with flour.

3. If you are working in a lawned garden, remove sods of turf to use elsewhere and dig a hole the same shape as your chosen container.

Installation

4. Lower the container into the hole and use a spirit level to check that that the lip is level. If it is not, remove the container and rectify.

5. Place the pump in the container and fix the semi-rigid tubing onto the outlet. Cut a hole in the centre of the plastic pot and position it upside-down over the pump. This will enable you to contain a greater volume of water in the reservoir than if stones were packed around the pump itself. It is also a good idea to drill three or four holes in the sides to allow the water to flow more easily between the pot and the reservoir.

6. Now pack river stones around the plastic pot to hide it and create a surface on which the pebbles can sit. Trim the tubing with a sharp knife to the required height. Alternatively, you could set a grid or piece of water-resistant board (fibre-cement, for instance) over the top of the container with a hole in the centre for the tubing, making allowance for water to run back into the reservoir.

7. Finally, pack the pebbles over the river stones, covering a wider circumference than that of the bowl.

STEP 5

STEP 2

STEP 3

STEP 6

The pebble fountain has been sited in lawn next to an attractive garden bed.

Connecting the fountain

8. You will, of course, need to plug the submersible pump into a power socket. If the feature is in the garden, some distance from the house, you will have to bury cable underground (*see* pages 30-31).

9. When the pump is operated with a fountain head fitting, a jet of water gushes into the air like a geyser.

10. If you wish, you may slot a different fountain head onto the tubing in order to change the effect altogether. The dome- or tulip-jet is always a favourite for pebble fountains.

STEP 9

STEP 10

JAPANESE FEATURE FOUNTAIN

This Japanese-style fountain, modelled on a traditional *shishi odoshi*, enhances a pebble garden planted with grasses, bamboo and suitable shrubs. There is nothing to stop you erecting it so that the water from the bamboo pipes flows into an appropriately designed koi pond. The green colour of bamboo will fade to a characteristic golden brown as it dries, creating a natural effect that complements the simple elements and shapes of this delightful fountain.

Materials
5 kg (11 lb) cement
20 kg (44 lb) sand
1 x 1 m x 80 mm (3 ft 3 in x 3¼ in)
    length bamboo
2 x 600 mm x 80 mm (2 ft x 3¼ in)
    lengths bamboo
3 x 450 mm x 80 mm

(1 ft 6 in x 3¼ in) lengths bamboo
1 x 260 mm x 10 mm (10 in x ⅜ in)
    galvanized hexagonal bolt with nut
8 washers
2 m (6 ft 6 in) natural fibre rope
string (optional)
1 x 1.5 m x 10 mm (5 ft x ⅜ in)
    flexible tubing

Preparation
1. This Japanese-style fountain can be incorporated with the previous project. First you should remove the grass around the reservoir of water. Then follow steps 1-4 for the Pebble Fountain (pages 76-77).

Assembling the bamboo feature
2. If you have cut your own bamboo, you will now have to saw it to size. Do this with a tenon saw, cutting off an angle of 45° at one end of both the 450 mm (1 ft 6 in) and the 1 m (3 ft 3 in) lengths of bamboo.

3. To work efficiently, you will have to ensure that there is a natural joint in the longest piece of bamboo, just ahead of where it is bolted (*see* illustration). Additional joints between this one and the angled end will have to be drilled out (using a wood drill bit) so that the weight of the water will cause the pivoted bamboo to see-saw. You may also have to drill into the second angled segment to feed through the tubing.

4. Drill holes in the remaining two 450 mm (1 ft 6 in) lengths, approximately 100 mm (4 in) from the top, and a hole in the 1 m (3 ft 3 in) length at a point about halfway. Also drill one of the 600 mm (2 ft) lengths to accommodate the tubing (*see* illustration).

Pebbles, grasses, ferns and the Japanese bamboo fountain create character and interest.

5. Bolt the three pieces of bamboo together as illustrated, sliding 4 washers between each piece to create two even gaps.

6. Cut holes in the two 600 mm (2 ft) lengths of bamboo to support the shorter horizontal length. These should be 150 mm (6 in) from the top of each one and the same diameter as the bamboo it will support (in this case 80 mm or 3¼ in). Install the fountain, by tying the three pieces together temporarily with string.

Installing the bamboo feature
7. Dig two foundation trenches measuring 250 mm x 250 mm x 150 mm (10 in x 10 in x 6 in), and position the bamboo so that the smaller horizontal section of the fountain constantly feeds the one below it with water. The longer, lower, pivoted side has a see-saw action which should spill into the pebble reservoir, while the pieces that are tied together act as a faucet. Use a spirit level to check that the four bamboo posts are standing absolutely upright.

8. Now mix the cement and sand in the ratio 1:4 and add water until it is smooth and porridge-like. There is no need to add stone, as this is a lightweight structure, although you can if you wish. Lift the

cement mixture with a spade and pour it into the two trenches. Compact it with the back of the spade. Double-check that the posts are still straight.

9. Place the pump in the reservoir bowl with one end of the tubing fixed to the outlet pipe. When the cement has set, push the tubing through the one 600 mm (2 ft) post. Lead the power cable to a waterproof socket box or lay underground conduit.

10. Replace the string with more sturdy, more attractive rope. Do this by crossing two pieces over on one side and securing

with a reef knot. Use string to neaten the ends if you wish. While you are doing this, use a spirit level to check that the horizontal faucet is straight.

11. River stones and pebbles are now set in position over the reservoir, as with the pebble fountain, except that you may want to spread the pebbles further, rather than creating a circular feature.

Finishing off
12. Fill the reservoir with water and plant around the feature with grasses, ferns or miniature bamboo.

STEP 3

STEP 8

CROSSING WATER

Bridges and stepping stones offer us the opportunity to cross water, in both aesthetic and practical ways. They also enable us to gain closer access to the water and to admire and enjoy it from a vantage point other than along its shores. Carefully planned and properly designed, these features will add interest and character to the area in which they are located.

An arched timber bridge leads over a stream into a grotto.

You may feel that a suitable place for a bridge or walkway is only the larger pond, natural river, stream, or water feature incorporating an island. This is not the case at all. Just two or three stepping stones leading through a modest pool or stream, or a little arched bridge across a koi pond will encourage you to approach the water and enjoy its pleasures. It may even provide that finishing touch.

Any existing style or design theme in the garden should determine the method used to bridge water. Stepping stones can have an Oriental feel about them, especially when organised in the traditional Japanese way. A simple, flat, wooden walkway extending across water will suit most informal layouts. A single log or railway sleeper is effective as a crossing medium where you do not want to detract from the natural effect of a waterway or stream. Conversely, an elaborate, arched bridge will be a feature in itself.

BRIDGES

When you include a bridge in your garden design, make sure that the type of structure you choose complements not only the water feature it will cross, but the surrounding environment as well. It should also be in proportion to the rest of the garden. It is therefore important to consider its dimensions carefully.

Height above the water is only a factor when boats need to pass under a bridge. A slightly raised design however will allow an enticing glimpse of the garden, as well as the water it crosses. While the simplest designs can be most effective, the inclusion of a couple of steps at either end will add both height and interest.

The width of the bridge will obviously determine the number of people who can use it at any one time. Relatively few contemporary gardens can accommodate a structure much broader than 900 mm (3 ft); the bridge featured in our step-by-step project is only 600 mm (2 ft) wide.

When estimating how long your bridge should be, it is essential that the structure crosses the water and also extends over solid ground. This is a visually pleasing and practical design approach, particularly where bank erosion could occur in later years and make the structure unsafe.

If railings are included (*see* Safety, page 83), the basic design of your structure will probably determine their characteristics. Some Oriental bridges feature quite elaborate lacquered wooden railings and latticework, although many simple Japanese bridges, built from stone or with wooden planks, traditionally have no railings at all. Structures found in rural settings are more likely to utilise straightforward timber handrails or even thick rope affixed to stout poles.

Even where handrails are not necessary for practical reasons, you may opt to incorporate them as a design feature, or to make the bridge look more substantial.

STEPPING STONES

Where a bridge is likely to appear intrusive, stepping stones are an obvious alternative. They are modest in size, relatively easy to construct or position, and can be used over a small or large expanse of water. Furthermore, stepping stones are an effective addition to both formal and informal water features, fitting whichever style you prefer.

Flat-topped rocks make very effective stepping stones and they should be well anchored in the soil, or even concreted into place for safety's sake. They fit the informal style well and may be used to cross streams, ponds or even a bog garden. Choose large rocks and space them evenly for ease of use.

If natural materials are scarce, simulated stone slabs may be set on top of brick piers to create a similar impression. This can be particularly effective if the similar looking material has been used around the edge of the pond.

Obviously man-made stepping stones, comprising tiles or slabs supported on plastered brick piers (*see* page 86) are more suited to formal water features. If tiles are used, avoid those with a glazed surface for safety reasons.

The materials you choose should be resistant to constant immersion in water and to frost if you live in a cold climate. Remember that stepping stones are easier to construct if the water feature is reasonably shallow. They should be built, or set in place, before the pond is filled with water which means that you may have to drain the water from an established pool before you begin.

Two strips of timber provide a visual link over a small patio pond.

A simple timber bridge spans a natural stream in a garden.

Two stout sleepers provide a safe and practical crossing point.

LOCATION

The most obvious place to position a bridge or stepping stones is where the contours of the pool suggest a natural crossing point. However, you may find it less visually intrusive to bridge a pond at one end, perhaps where a natural bog garden crosses it, rather than obstruct the view of the water.

An existing pathway leading to the water might suggest an obvious place to cross. Or, construct a bridge where you choose and extend an established path along the bank of the water feature to meet it.

Although it is not essential for a bridge or stepping stones to lead anywhere at all, there is little point in including them in your design if they do not encourage people to cross, or at least draw them closer to the water feature.

MATERIALS

Choice of materials will relate primarily to safety, although budget, finish and effect will also be important factors.

Timber is a common choice for all types of bridges, but generally should be avoided when it comes to stepping stones. Logs and sliced tree trunks set in the water will quickly become mossy and slippery, creating a dangerous walkway.

An attractive Japanese-style bridge leads across an expansive koi pond to the entrance of the house.

Concrete is a useful material, which may be cast *in situ* (*see* page 22), and used in conjunction with other finishes such as stone or other pre-cast products.

Although stone has been used to construct bridges for many centuries, the skills required, as well as the scarcity of natural stone in many areas, make this a much less usual option for the average garden. Large, flat-topped stones may be used successfully as stepping stones.

SAFETY

While water in the garden is a potential hazard, especially for young children (*see* page 9), a badly-built bridge or unstable stepping stones will exacerbate this danger. It is vital that all bridges are sturdy and properly built and that anything used to traverse water is as non-slip as possible.

Of course, handrails are recommended in any situation which may be potentially dangerous: for instance, where a high bridge spans a river or where children and elderly people are likely to be at risk.

Stepping stones below the water level, will tend to attract algae and become slippery, creating a crossing as dangerous as a bridge without handrails. It is therefore extremely important to have a reasonably rough surface underfoot.

A practical timber and brick bridge allows vehicles to cross the stream.

A rustic timber bridge made from split poles is a feature in this water garden.

WOODEN BRIDGE

A simple wooden bridge can be both practical and attractive, adding to the appeal of most water gardens. This design incorporates straightforward handrails and a slightly arched walkway. A properly treated softwood bridge, like this one, will give you many years of pleasure, although a hardwood will be more resistant to rot and weathering.

The walkway of the structure featured here was made from inexpensive pine split poles planed to form planks which are slightly rounded on one side. Since these are not standard in all saw mills, the materials list specifies ordinary planed planks of the same size. All the timber used should be planed all round (PAR) and treated; you may need to adapt timber dimensions slightly, depending on what is available in your area.

STEP 2

Materials

1 x 3 m x 150 mm x 50 mm (10 ft x 6 in x 2 in) length timber for bearers

6 x 900 mm x 76 mm x 38 mm (3 ft x 3 in x 1½ in) for uprights

22 x 600 mm x 70 mm x 22 mm (2 ft x 2 ¾ in x ¾ in) walkway planks

4 x 900 mm x 76 mm x 25 mm (3 ft x 3 in x 1 in) handrails

6 x 70 mm (2¾ in) wire nails

12 x 70 mm x 6 mm (2¾ in x ¼ in) galvanised coach screws

16 x 50 mm x 4 mm (2 in x ⅛ in) cross-head screws

88 x 40 mm (1½ in) ring shanked nails or self-tapping screws

Preparation

1. The first step is to cut all the required timber to size and make sure you have sufficient screws and nails for the project. Also assemble your tools.

2. While most of the lengths are straight-forward to cut, the two bearers, which are sawn from a 3 m (10 ft) long piece of wood, must be curved, and this is a little more complicated. Mark out the first bearer by knocking two nails partially into the wood 1.5 m (5 ft) apart, slightly in from one end and from the bottom edge to

A natural, trickling stream meanders through an undeveloped country garden.

facilitate cutting. Now measure the central point between them and knock in a third nail, just in from the opposite edge. Then bend a thin strip of pliable wood between the nails to enable you to draw a curve with ease. Draw a second curved line 75 mm (3 in) below this, making sure the width of the bearer is even. You can use additional nails to support the strip of wood if you wish.

3. Using a jigsaw, cut along the lines you have drawn. Do not cut the length of wood in half as you will need the overlap in the centre.

4. Now use the first bearer as a template for the second bearer, drawing around it to mark your cutting line.

STEP 3

STEP 1

STEP 5

STEP 6

STEP 8

STEP 10

Construction

5. Nail two straight lengths of timber to the underside of each bearer. These will act as temporary supports and will be removed once the structure is complete. Note that neither these lengths of wood, nor the nails, are included in the list of materials. Use ordinary wire nails and any suitable scraps of timber.

6. Turn one of the bearers on its side and position three of the uprights as indicated, with 150 mm (4 in) of each outer one extending below the bearers. These extensions can be set into the ground later for added stability. The bottom of the central upright timber should be flush with the lower edge of the curved bearer. Make sure all three lengths of wood are absolutely straight and parallel with one another, before knocking in wire nails to hold them in place. Check again that they are vertical, and then secure with two coach screws at the base of each upright. It helps to use a batten under the uprights to support them while you are working; this piece of wood does not, however, form part of the structure.

7. Repeat the procedure described in step 6, using the second bearer and all of the remaining uprights.

8. With the temporary slats still nailed to them, position the two bearers upright on a flat surface 600 mm (2 ft) apart. Nail the planks to the upper surface of the bearers with ring shanked nails; or use self-tapping screws (which are also hammered in).

9. Measure the six upright posts and trim them to the desired height with a jigsaw. You will achieve a good balance if the centre lengths are 700 mm (2 ft 4 in), and the outer ones about 830 mm (2 ft 9 in) at their longest point which includes the 150 mm (4 in) extensions. Then trim the upper ends of the uprights at a slight angle (*see* illustration) with a jigsaw or tenon saw, so that the handrails will fit snugly.

10. Using the 16 Phillips head screws and an appropriate screwdriver, secure the handrail to the upright posts. Take care to ensure that the upright timbers remain completely straight.

Finishing

11. Sand rough edges, rounding the ends of the handrails if you wish, and remove the temporary slats. Finally, apply a sealer following the manufacturer's instructions.

The bridge is both functional and attractive.

SIMPLE STEPPING STONES

Designed to allow access from the garden to a stairway built alongside the house, these stepping stones are topped with non-slip marble tiles. Supporting piers 500 mm (1 ft 8 in) high have been made with bricks and mortar, while the surface matches adjacent paving and is level with it. For convenience, one stepping stone abuts the stairway, but this is not essential. Although the finish here is essentially formal, the basic step-by-step instructions may be adapted for just about any man-made stepping stones. Materials and DIY instructions for the pool are not included in this project.

A stepping stone is attached to the stairway.

5. Mix cement and sand in the ratio 1:3, using two bags of cement. For each pier measuring approximately 800 mm x 320 mm (2 ft 8 in x 1¼ in) you will need 48 to 63 bricks. If fewer bricks are used you will need to fill the central cavity with hardcore or concrete before the tops can be tiled.

6. Lay the bricks as shown in figure 3 with additional bricks in between them if you wish. Make absolutely certain that the corners are at 90°, using a builder's square to check this frequently. Every brick course must bond with the next, so allow the bricks in each successive course to overlap those below by half (*see* figure 1.).

7. For 500 mm (1 ft 8 in) high piers, you will need to build up six courses. Corner blocks (*see* page 11) and a builder's line will help ensure that each course is even. If the upper level of the stepping stones is not even, you will find it difficult to walk across them, so also use a gauge rod to maintain equal mortar joints.

Materials
This project allows for construction of five rectangular stepping stones approximately 800 mm x 320 mm (2 ft 8 in x 1 ft) equally spaced across a 2.24 m (7 ft 4 in) wide pool.
288-315 bricks
12½ x 320 mm x 320 mm (1 ft x 1 ft) tiles
125 kg (275 lb) cement
390 kg (0.3 cu yd) sand
waterproofing agent (optional)
15 litres (3¼ gal) rubberised bitumen sealer

Preparation
1. You will need a solid foundation for the stepping stones. For this reason it is best to build your pond with bricks and mortar or to construct a concrete shell as described in previous projects (*see* pages 40 and 42). It is possible to build stepping stones in a liner pond (*see* figure 2), but there is a real danger that you will puncture the plastic during construction.

2. Allow the concrete shell or foundation to set before you start laying the bricks.

3. If you are building stepping stones in an existing pond, drain the water first and scrub the inner shell to get rid of algae and other plant growth.

Brickwork
4. Measure out the position of the stepping stones and mark these on the concrete with chalk or loose bricks.

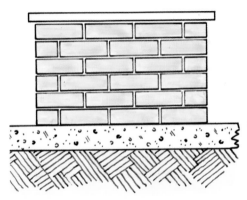

Figure 1.
One of the project stepping stones.

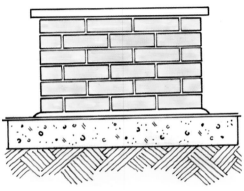

Figure 2.
Stepping stone on flexible liner.

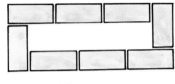

Courses 1,3,5

Figure 3.
Courses 2,4,6

Plastering or rendering

8. Once you have completed the brick-work, allow the mortar to set for at least 24 hours. Your plaster or render should be mixed in exactly the same ratio as the mortar used previously. You can add a non-toxic plasticiser (*see* page 14) to make the mixture more cohesive, but avoid lime especially if you plan to stock the pool with fish. It is a good idea to add a little waterproofing agent.

9. It is best to use a screed board to hold the mixture while you work. Lay the render on with a plasterer's trowel, applying pressure so that it sticks to the surface. When you have roughly plastered all six of the piers, go back to the first one and smooth it with a plasterer's float. Use a corner trowel for neat corners.

Tiling

10. If you plan to use an adhesive to set the tiles in place, you must wait for a few days until the render has set. Alternatively, you can use a little of the plaster/render mix, in which case you will not have to wait before putting the tiles on top of the piers, but work carefully or your handi-work could be ruined. Instead of the usual tile adhesive, simply spread a little of your mixed render on the back of the tiles, using a notched trowel to form ridges to aid adhesion. Push them into place and knock gently with a rubber mallet to level them.

11. If you are using the size tile specified, you will need 2½ tiles for the top of each pier, which means some tile cutting. The simplest way to do this is with a tile-cutting machine. First mark the cutting line with a pencil and then score the sur-face of the tile. Bring the handle of the machine down firmly to cut the tile. If you are using reconstituted stone or quarry tiles, you will have to use an angle grinder.

12. If you used a tile adhesive to set the tiles, allow this to dry before grouting the joints. Alternatively, rub a little of the plas-ter mix into the gaps between the tiles.

Finishing

13. Do not allow the plaster/render coat to dry out too quickly. Damp it down with a fine spray of water from the garden hose once or twice a day, for a few days, to help it cure thoroughly.

14. Seal the supporting piers of the step-ping stones with a rubberised bitumen sealer or suitable polyurethane when you seal the pond shell.

Marble tiles give the stepping stones a sophisticated finish which complements patios.

SMALL WATER FEATURES

For those who do not have the time or space to construct a lavish water garden, there are numerous small feature ideas which will transform dull corners of the patio or garden. These range from a simple stone basin to small spurting ornaments which may be part of a larger feature. The projects are ideal for amateurs and can be tackled in a single weekend.

Plain, but not ordinary, this feature is perfect for the smaller patio.

An ingenious feature utilises African pots and the concept of a pebble garden.

Many small water features may be part of a larger water garden, but most will stand on their own, enlivening unexciting patios and uninteresting corners of the garden. A little tub or bowl filled with water can sparkle with life, while a miniature pond will capture interesting reflections.

Various materials may be used to create small features, from tubs and basins to bamboo and old railway sleepers. Pumps and fountain fittings can be used although they are not essential.

It may seem unnecessary to plan a small feature as carefully as a full-scale water garden, but it is worth assessing the style of the finished design. Most will fit into any outdoor location, but some might look a bit out of place. On the other hand, a little contrast can be invigorating.

The first step is to decide what you want. All kinds of containers, such as barrels, basins and troughs, may be converted into mini-ponds. Suitability is determined largely by durability and impermeability of the vessel, and additional waterproofing (see page 17) may be necessary. It is also important that they are non-toxic and will not corrode over time. Before you get to work, check what was stored in the container previously; anything with poisonous preservatives or oil should be avoided.

While you will want to position an attractive container where it can be seen, more ordinary vessels may be buried in the ground to create a miniature pond. You could sink a few more containers alongside it and convert them into small 'bog gardens'. Just remember to drill a few holes in the base of those to be planted, and be sure to keep the soil moist.

A mini-pond will enable you to have a water feature in the tiniest of areas. Most of these are too small for fish, but they can be effectively planted with aquatics.

A word of warning: small water features are not necessarily safer. Remember that babies and toddlers have been known to drown in a bucket of water.

A pre-cast fountain feature is the focal point of this herb and flower garden.

A mass of plants add interest to a pre-cast concrete fountain feature.

The safest water features for small children are those which incorporate hidden reservoirs of water. A pebble fountain (*see* page 76) or millstone feature are two popular options. The water and a pump are contained underground in a pre-cast receptacle. The surface is covered with the millstone and/or pebbles and the water pumped through pipework to the surface. Fountain heads may also be used, and a tulip- or dome-jet is particularly attractive.

Bamboo is another useful material for the smaller feature, especially when a Japanese-style effect is required. There are several possibilities ranging from the traditional *tsukabai*, made with bamboo pipework and a hollowed stone or water basin, to pivoted pouring devices originally designed to frighten deer and other animals (*shishi-odoshi*). Both pour a constant trickle of water through hollowed bamboo, although the *tsukabai* is static.

A number of ingenious designs are possible on a small scale. Exploit the hidden reservoir concept and pump water behind a bush or boulder and into a pot which spills onto pebbles or into a small pond below. Or pump it up behind logs or railway sleepers set upright in the ground, allowing the water to trickle back over the wood.

You can set an attractive pond ornament over the tiniest pool, drawing up the water with a small submersible pump, so that the ornament becomes the focus rather than the water.

A handmade ceramic fountain is a simple but effective water feature.

FLOWING URN

An ordinary urn, manufactured for pot plants, makes an attractive water feature in a compact border bed. It takes up little space and introduces the sight and sound of trickling water. Although various containers may be used, a shaped vessel is preferable. You will need to provide or construct a reservoir of water which is hidden beneath the urn. It is essential that this is designed to accommodate the necessary pipework which will enable the water to flow back under the container. Note that the diameters given for this project relate to the upper openings of containers.

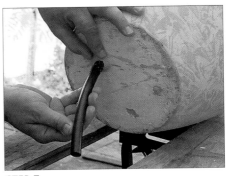
STEP 7

STEP 8

Materials

urn approximately 250 mm (10 in) in diameter, 430 mm (1 ft 5in) high

container approximately 560 mm (1 ft 10 in) in diameter, 310 mm (1 ft) high

plastic pot, 200 mm (8 in) in diameter, 180 mm (7 in) high

1 x 600 mm x 12 mm (2 ft x ½ in) semi-rigid tubing

1 x submersible pump, with 1.4 m (4 ft 6 in) water head

river stones

Preparation

1. The first step is to ensure that any pre-cast container you plan to use as the reservoir is absolutely waterproof. If necessary plug up any holes and seal the interior surface. The reservoir here is a planter sold for small cacti displays. Made from fibrecement, it is manufactured with a hole in the base for drainage. It is an ideal shape for this feature, as the upper diameter is considerably wider than the base which, in turn, is the same size as the plastic pot. It is also quite simple to fill any drainage hole with a two-part epoxy putty.

2. Having decided where to site your flowing urn feature, place the waterproof container upside down and mark its upper diameter with flour or chalk.

3. Dig a 310 mm (1 ft) deep hole. If you are using a similar-shaped container, try to slope the walls to avoid unnecessary excavation.

STEP 4

Installation

4. Place the container in the hole you have dug and use a spirit level to check that it is level. Fill gaps with soil and compact .

5. Cut a hole in the bottom of your plastic plant pot to accommodate the pipework. Put the pump on the base of the waterproof container and place the pot upside down over it.

6. The urn used must also be waterproof, except for the hole you need for the pipework. Seal any other holes with epoxy putty and allow to dry thoroughly. Paint the container if you wish. This one has a rag-rolled finish in shades of terracotta.

7. You will need to drill a hole in the bottom of the urn with a 16 mm (⅝ in) diameter to accommodate tubing with a 12 mm (½ in) bore. Push the tubing through the hole so it extends almost to the top of the urn. Use two-part epoxy putty to keep it in place and seal around the tube.

8. Position the urn on the plastic pot so that the tubing extends through it, and join the tubing to the pump connection. Make sure the pot and urn are level.

Finishing off

9. Fill the bottom container with water and place river stones around the feature to disguise the arrangement below. Note that some of the rocks will inevitably be positioned in the reservoir.

10. Fill the urn with water, connect the power and switch it on to start the water flowing.

Water trickles and flows over the edges of the urn onto the rocks below. With time, moss and algae will collect on both rocks and container, giving the feature a less contrived feel.

DECORATIVE POND

Although many small water features look artificial, it is possible to create a natural-looking pond on a very small scale. This has the appearance of rock and you can choose any simulated stone product or even a small fibreglass shell. In some places, thermoplastic liners are manufactured to look like simulated rock. Installation is simple and a small water feature can be completed within hours. The secret is to sink the pond into the ground so that it looks as though it has occured naturally, and then to plant right up to the rim of the feature.

STEP 4

4. The next step is to backfill around the pond and to compact the soil, filling all visible gaps so that it sits firmly in place.

Finishing off
5. A rock-faced pond like the one shown here, does not require an edging. It will look more natural, however, if you plant right up to the edge with groundcover. If you are using a shell which is not as realistic, you can edge the pond with simulated stone slabs or smallish rocks to hide the rim.

6. Fill the mini-pond with water to enjoy the effect you have created.

Materials
For a pre-cast pond with a maximum diameter of 740 mm (2 ft 6 in):
A suitable pre-cast shell

Preparation
1. It is essential that the ground into which you sink your pre-cast pond is absolutely level. You can rectify slight undulations with soil dug out from the hole, but a pond this small is not suitable for sloping or uneven ground.

Installation
2. Dig a hole slightly larger than the shell, taking the irregular shape into account. Use a spirit level to check that the base of the hole is flat and level.

3. Place the shell into the hole and make sure it is level. If necessary, use a long, straight-edged piece of wood under the spirit level.

STEP 2

STEP 3

Within a few hours the transformation is complete. The ground cover has been re-established around the pond which is just big enough to support a few goldfish and floating aquatic plants

PLANTER CASCADE

Small patio features often benefit from the addition of potted plants. This mini-cascade is no exception, and look-alike planters have been used to contain both water and plants. Although the receptacles may be made of various materials, they should be geometric and regular in shape. Sizes may be different to those illustrated, provided they fit together attractively. Those which hold water must be absolutely waterproof, while the planted containers should have holes for drainage.

STEP 6

STEP 7

Materials
- 4 x troughs 600 mm x 600 mm x 200 mm (2 ft x 2 ft x 8 in)
- 2 x planters 380 mm x 380 mm x 380 mm (1 ft 3 in x 1 ft 3 in x 1 ft 3 in)
- 2 x planters 380 mm x 380 mm x 580 mm (1 ft 3 in x 1 ft 3 in x 2 ft)
- 48 bricks
- 1 x 200 mm x 12 mm (8 in x ½ in) semi-rigid tubing
- 1 x 1.5 m x 10 mm (5 ft x ⅜ in) flexible tubing
- 5 x 100 mm x 16 mm (4 in x ⅝ in) rigid PVC pipe
- 1 x submersible pump, with 1.4 m (4 ft 6 in) water head

Preparation
1. Seal the drainage holes in three of the troughs with a two-part epoxy putty.

2. Trim the ends of the PVC pipe at an angle to form a spout as shown on page 74. Give the rough edges a light sanding.

3. To accommodate the pipe, you will need to drill holes in two of the sealed troughs, 25 mm (1 in) below the rim and at 200 mm (8 in) centres apart. In the fourth trough (which is to be used as a planter), drill one central hole for the PVC spout. Presuming you are using PVC with a 16 mm (⅝ in) bore, all these holes should be about 20 mm (¾ in) in diameter.

4. Position the five pieces of pipe in the holes and secure with epoxy putty. Make sure they are all level or the water will not flow through evenly.

5. When the putty is dry, you can paint the troughs if you wish. Decorate the planters at the same time.

Installation
6. Place the loose bricks as indicated to provide a stepped support for the troughs. If you are using containers with different dimensions, this arrangement will have to be altered. Make sure the bricks are secure and level.

7. Now you can position the water troughs on the bricks, with the spoutless container on the ground. Use a spirit level lengthwise on each one to ensure they are level. It is easier to make adjustments now than when they are full of water.

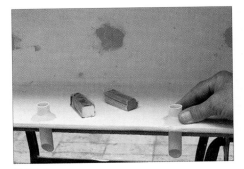
STEP 4

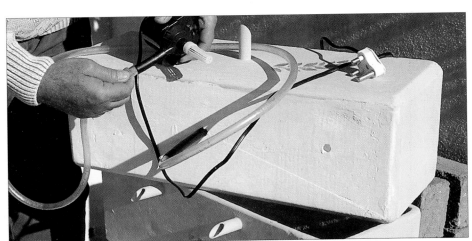
STEP 8

Fitting the pump

8. You will probably need to drill a 16 mm (⅝ in) hole in the bottom of the top trough so that you can push the semi-rigid tubing through it and into the top spout. Join the other end to the flexible tubing, which is, in turn, attached to the pump.

9. When you position the top trough, make sure the tubing falls through the gap in the bricks so that you can lead it out through one side. Position the pump in the bottom trough.

Finishing off

10. Now you can position the planters, with the highest two at the back. Once they are planted, you will be unlikely to notice the tubing.

11. Fill the troughs with water and plug the pump into a suitably waterproofed outdoor socket, or into the nearest indoor socket. Switch on the power and enjoy the fruits of your labour.

The corner of an ordinary patio lacks life and vitality.

The cascade water feature adds colour and interest to the patio, inviting one to linger a little longer.

GLOSSARY

Aggregate Described as being 'fine' or 'coarse', aggregate is added to cement and water to give bulk to concrete and mortar mixes. The most usual forms are sand (fine) and crushed stone (coarse).

Batching Method of measuring materials for one batch of concrete, mortar or render. All batching in this book is by volume.

Batten Lengths of timber commonly used as part of a roof structure.

Bentonite Natural, montmorillonite clay mined for a wide variety of uses in industry and as a clarifying agent. Packaged in powder form with various additives (forming hydrous aluminium silicate) for use as a sealant for ponds and dams.

Bog Area of wet spongy ground.

Bond Method used to strengthen and hold brick walls together. Bricks are laid in various patterns to form different bonds.

Bore Hollow part of piping; term used in relation to internal diameter.

Butyl rubber A synthetic rubber used to line ponds and pools.

Chicken-wire Wire netting with a hexagonal mesh, traditionally used to fence-in chickens. Useful for DIY concrete ponds.

Clay puddling Traditional method used to seal ponds with impervious clay.

Cobble Rounded stone used to form a path, patio or road surface. Man-made cobbles are usually regular in shape and more like *setts* (*see* below).

Course A continuous row of bricks. Several courses form a wall.

Curing Keeping concrete or mortar moist to ensure a chemical reaction which gives it strength as it hardens.

Datum point A known point which is utilised to attain levels; for instance around the upper surface of a pond.

Dressed stone Stone that has been cut to create a reasonably smooth surface which is suitable for building.

EPDM Relatively inexpensive rubber made from an ethylene propylene polymer.

Facebrick Clay or concrete brick manufactured for use without plaster.

Fibrecement Material composed of cement, organic fibres and sometimes a small percentage of asbestos, which can be moulded to form pond shells, fountain features and pot plant containers.

Float Process used to smooth floor screeds or rendered walls.

Formwork Shuttering used to form a profile which holds wet concrete cast *in situ*.

French drain Drain filled with hardcore to allow water to drain through.

GRC Glassfibre reinforced cement used to mould architectural features and various products including fake rocks.

Gypsum plaster An internal plaster finish, containing hydrated calcium sulphate, used on both bare and rendered walls. Certain gypsum plasters (e.g. cretestone), are used to skim ceilings and plasterboard.

Hardcore Various materials including broken bricks, or stones used to improve drainage or compacted to form a well-drained sub-base beneath concrete.

Hardwood Botanical classification identifying broad-leafed species of tree.

Hot tub Forerunner of acrylic hot-water spas, hot tubs are traditionally made from Californian redwood and incorporate all the fittings found in spas.

Level Flat horizontal plane. Various instruments enable you to ensure that walls and other surfaces are flat and level.

Marbelite A mixture of white cement and granular marble dust used to plaster the internal shell of swimming pools.

Mortar Mixture of cement, sand and water used to bond bricks when building a wall or other structure.

Peatbog Bog composed of soil and vegetable matter with a high acid content.

pH Degree of acidity or alkalinity of pool water, measured on a scale from 0-14.

Piling Post or heavy beam driven into soft sand to support a deck, bridge or other structure. For pile foundations, holes are bored into the ground and then filled with reinforced concrete.

Plaster A protective coating applied to bare brick or cement block walls. Some people refer to plaster as a cement and sand mixture (*see Render*), in parts of the world, it refers only to gypsum plasters.

Plumb Flat, vertical plane.

Polyethylene Polymerized material, including polythene, often referred to as 'plastic'. May be manufactured as sheeting or moulded to various shapes.

Prime Procedure used to make some pumps start working. Certain surfaces must also be primed – or prepared – before they can be painted.

PVC Commonly used abbreviation for polyvinyl chloride, a thermoplastic made from a polymer of vinyl chloride. Available in both sheet and moulded forms.

Render A coat of mortar (sometimes referred to as 'plaster') generally applied to exterior walls. There are various rendered finishes, although smooth stucco is probably the most common.

Setts A small block of stone (traditionally granite) used for paving.

Screed A smooth mortar layer spread over concrete to create a flat surface.

Shuttering Framework of wood or steel, erected as a temporary support for concrete to be cast on site.

Softwood Botanical specification identifying conifers.

Square Of square or rectangular shape. To ensure a structure is square, its corners must be at right-angles (90°).

Water head The height a pump can spurt from the surface of the water in a pond or pool (*see* Fountains, page 66).

LIST OF SUPPLIERS

UNITED KINGDOM

Blagdon Water Garden Products Ltd
Bristol Road
Bridgwater
Somerset TA6 4AW

Tel: 01278 446464

B & Q plc
Portswood House
Hampshire Corporate Park
Chandlers Ford
Eastleigh
Hants S05 3YX
(Branches throughout the UK)

Tel: 01703 256256

The Water Gardener Magazine
9 Tufton Street
Ashford
Kent TN23 1QN

Tel: 01233 621877

Do-It-All
Falcon House
The Minories
Dudley
West Midlands DY2 8PG

Tel: 01384 456456

Homebase Ltd
Beddington House
Wallington
Surrey

Tel: 0181 784 7200

Travis Perkins
Lodge Way House
Lodge Way
Harlestone Road
Northampton
NN7 7UG

Tel: 01604 752424

Great Mills
RNC House
Paulton
Bristol
BS18 5SX
(Branches throughout the UK)

Tel: 01761 416034

Surrey Water Gardens
Clandon Park
Clandon
Nr Guildford
Surrey

Tel: 01483 224822

Aquatek
33 Bruce Grove
North Watford
WD2 5AQ

Tel: 01923 246312

Waterworld
Kingswood Nurseries
Bullsmoor Lane
Enfield
EN1 4SF

Tel: 01992 761587

Aqualand
15 Brunswick Street
Morley
Leeds LS27 9DJ

Tel: 01532 522717

NEW ZEALAND

Natural Habitats
240 Orakei Road, Auckland

Tel: 529 0192

Nature Zone
184 Old Titiransa Road
Auckland

Tel: 817 6064

About Landscaping
PO Box 114
Takanini, Auckland

Tel: 524 3666

Daniel Tohill
401 Richmond Road
Grey Lynn, Auckland

Tel: 379 5459

Dr Spruce
Landscaper, Auckland

Tel: 486 1959

AUSTRALIA

Adelaide Watergardens
4 Bredbo Street
Lonsdale SA 5160

Tel: 08 384 5344

H & H Pond Shops
325 Harborne Street
Osborne Park WA 6017

Tel: 09 242 5755

Gro 'N' Flo Garden Supplies
131 Bunya Road
Arana Hills
Queensland 4054

Tel: 07 851 1221

Whitehouse Gardens
388 Springvale Road
Forest Hill
Victoria 3131

Tel: 03 877 1430

INDEX